Little Me BIG Business

Little Me
BIG
Business

How to Grow Your Small Business,
Increase Your Profits and Go Global
(in Your Pajamas)

Nadia Finer

NEW YORK

LONDON • NASHVILLE • MELBOURNE • VANCOUVER

Little Me BIG Business
How to Grow Your Small Business, Increase Your Profits and Go Global (in Your Pajamas)

© 2019 **Nadia Finer**

Published in New York, New York, by Morgan James Publishing. Morgan James is a trademark of Morgan James, LLC. www.MorganJamesPublishing.com

The Morgan James Speakers Group can bring authors to your live event. For more information or to book an event visit The Morgan James Speakers Group at www.TheMorganJamesSpeakersGroup.com.

ISBN 978-1-68350-851-9 paperback
ISBN 978-1-68350-852-6 eBook
Library of Congress Control Number: 2017960663

Cover Design by:
Rachel Lopez
www.r2cdesign.com

Interior Design by:
Bonnie Bushman
The Whole Caboodle Graphic Design

In an effort to support local communities, raise awareness and funds, Morgan James Publishing donates a percentage of all book sales for the life of each book to Habitat for Humanity Peninsula and Greater Williamsburg.

Get involved today! Visit
www.MorganJamesBuilds.com

Table of Contents

Little Me BIG Business

You have ambitions to go big in your business. You want to work with people all over the world, become known for what you do, to build a tribe, to spread your message and help more people. You want to make more money!

But at the same time you want to stay small. You like being a lone ranger. You love working from home. You want your business to work around your life. You need that flexibility and you love being in control.

How can you achieve one, without losing the other?

Don't despair. It is possible to build a big business with only little you in charge. And here's how.

Stop Playing Small

I bent my knees and took a deep breath. A rather unladylike grunt burst from my mouth. I attempted to lift my suitcase onto the bus before it drove off without me. As my vertebrae pinged I could feel my spinal cord begging me to give up and go home.

I was on the way to sell jewellery and gifts at the offices of a big bank in London. My friend and I had come up with idea of creating a collection of British-made jewellery and gifts and selling it to well-paid city workers. It was the early days of e-commerce and we couldn't afford the thousands of dollars needed to build an ecommerce site, so we kept it old school and schlepped around thousands of dollars of silver and silk and precious stones, setting up our stall in offices across the city.

Squeezing my sweaty body and super-heavy luggage onto the bus in rush hour, and dodging the daggers of the professional people in their pristine suits, was par for the course.

I knew running a business was going to be tough, but I wasn't prepared for this.

Sure, I'd had a lot of fun creating a brand and sourcing a range of gorgeous products. I'd learned a lot about selling, about curating a collection, about creating an offering that gave people what they want at a price they were willing to pay.

But that day, as I crammed myself into a filthy corner of the bus, hot, stressed and surrounded by irritated commuters, it occurred to me that I wanted something bigger from my life.

It wasn't enough for me to be working this hard to sell a couple of things. And I didn't want to get so sweaty doing it! I didn't want to be limited by the bus route or the size of suitcase I could carry. I wanted to be bigger. I wanted to make more people happy, not just the odd one here and there. I didn't want to make a few dollars, just enough to cover my costs. I wanted more than that.

The trouble was, I hadn't quite worked out how. Over the next few years I became obsessed with scale. Surely it was possible to build a business of my own that was fun and would also make money without giving me a hernia?

But this was not the first or last time I would create a business that felt more like a prison than the key to my future financial freedom.

"You're playing small. It's pathetic!"

I couldn't believe what I was hearing. Sneering, scornful derision from a colleague, someone who was supposed to be working with me to grow my fledgling PR agency business.

The aggression in her voice was ugly. I could see her eyes bulging, veins throbbing, spit flying through the air, even over the phone.

"You're holding us back," she said.

My head was spinning. What was happening here? Where had this even come from?

This was the business I had started on my own. My business. My idea.

I was pacing up and down my kitchen in pajamas and slippers, palms sweating as I listened to this tirade of abuse. I could feel everything I'd worked for come crumbling down around me.

"This is nothing more than a lifestyle business."

Boom.

It was like living through an episode of Shark Tank. She may as well have said. "I'm out."

A lifestyle business. To her this was the ultimate insult. To her it meant; you're lacking in ambition, sat at home, working from the kitchen table, knitting yoghurt; a talentless, feckless loser just keeping yourself busy and destined never to make any money.

My mind wandered again. Must pay attention. I gave myself a virtual shake and snapped back into the conversation, where more vicious words were flying. My ear, pressed hard against the phone, burned. The handset felt like it was about to spontaneously combust and blow my eyebrows clean off.

And then the clincher.

"Nobody takes you seriously, you're a joke."

Bam. A sharp left hook to the cheekbone.

"Because you're a mom and you only work part-time."

Where was this heading exactly?

"…You don't deserve to get paid the same as me."

I felt a molten volcano of rage rise up within me. The worm was turning. (That meant I was the worm; not ideal, but for now it would have to do.)

This wasn't happening to me. Absolutely not. Not after all that hard work.

I cleared my throat, took a breath and a steely voice I didn't recognize at all said, "It's over. You can expect to hear from my lawyer."

Admittedly, that comeback heralded all kinds of mayhem and stress, kicking off a six-month legal wrangle worthy of its own box set. But it certainly felt good to say. For that split second I stood tall, slippers replaced with virtual heels, a sharp suit, pointy shoulder pads and bouffy hair. In your face!

I put down the phone, hand shaking, and started to cry. This wasn't the plan. In fact, it was so far removed from the plan, I was lost in a forest without a sat nav, or even a map, car broken down, phone battery dead and a creepy hitchhiker with murderous intentions for company.

What really bothered me wasn't the shouting. It was the thought that she might be right.

What if I really was thinking small? A small-time player with small ambitions and smaller talent? This was the fear that had haunted me all my life.

You see, I had always dreamed of running a successful business, but there was a pesky little voice in my head holding me back. Actually, that little voice wasn't just in my head.

All my life I've had a little voice. Really little. Like, 8 years old little.

As a kid I was sent off to all kinds of elocution lessons to help me channel my inner Margaret Thatcher and get some gravelly gravitas. Talk about giving a girl a complex.

Imagine, being "encouraged" to spend hours laying on the floor like Colin Firth in the King's Speech, breathing deeply into my stomach in an attempt to transform my tone.

Despite the breathing exercises, my voice stayed resolutely little. In general, it doesn't bother me. It has its advantages; I could run some kind of dodgy phone sex line if I was ever particularly strapped for cash; the guys at the local Thai take-away know it's me when I ring up; I get what I want when I complain about something and, of course, I'm truly excellent at swearing; bloody brilliant, in fact.

But while my little voice might be perfect for cartoon voice-over work, it's always made me feel insecure; like people wouldn't take me seriously.

Hardly surprising, given that roughly once a week, when someone calls our house, they hear my voice, get confused, take an uncomfortably long pause, and then ask to speak to my mom.

I am the mom!

And of course, professionally, it's been a bit of a problem.

One ex-boss of mine announced to a client, "she might sound like a little girl, but she's got a big brain." Er, thanks?

I get shy. I don't like showing off, bragging or even humble bragging. And given half the chance I'd hide at home behind my computer. It's not the best trait for a would-be entrepreneur.

And now this trusted college was confirming my worst fears. Maybe because I'd always felt secretly small, being called on it really pushed my buttons!

And even worse, while I was scared I was playing it small, at the same time I wasn't even really sure I wanted to go big. Not in the way this person was suggesting.

I wasn't interested in a big team with huge corporate clients, investors, fancy serviced offices, pitches and oodles of schmoozing.

The only person I'd ever been trying to impress was me. I'd left a corporate 9-to-5 to start this business, and I didn't want to build my own corporate rat race to replace the old one.

But despite all that, my grasp on my business was weakening. We'd taken on employees, viewed posh offices, had regular high-pressure meetings in London. My phone was super-glued to my ear as

I dashed back and forth, pulse racing, sweat dripping down the back of my silk blouse.

Things were getting out of hand and I was falling out of love with the business I'd created.

I was distracted, stressed and unhappy. This wasn't what I had in mind when I started out. My business was meant to work around my life, not destroy it from the inside like a silent assassin.

Wanting a small business doesn't mean thinking small

I'm an entrepreneur. And I also happen to be mom to one fur baby and one rather less furry, soccer-mad, string bean. I'm a wife, daughter, sister, granddaughter and friend. There's a lot of stuff going on in my life.

To make matters more complex, the length of my work day can optimistically be described as brief. I've had longer lasting baths! In fact, on occasion I've taken a power nap, only to wake up and find it's over. I literally blinked and missed it.

But I didn't just want a hobby business. I wasn't playing around. My ideal business was something that would have a big impact, that would be fulfilling and important, but that would also fit into my life, not take it over.

Surely there had to be a smarter, less stressful way; a way to stay small but create a big-impact business, one that scales, in just a few hours a day ... from the comfort of my sofa?

I was determined to prove it could be done.

So I closed my agency business before it sucked all the joy out of my life, but alas, the big answer to my question didn't immediately present itself. There was no extreme makeover. No big reveal. Sorry!

The truth is, before I could be any use to anyone or anything I had scrape myself up off the floor and flomp onto the sofa, where I spent many months. Never has one person watched so much daytime TV.

Finally, the ideas started to flow, but man, they were not good! I hopped from one random idea to another, clutching at flimsy opportunities that would sink without a trace.

My judgment had taken a battering. It took me a few months to realize, for example, that a business reviewing French movies was not going to bring in the big bucks. Duh. Turns out, brainstorming with a broken heart leads you down some very strange paths indeed.

Eventually, inspiration struck. And the inspiration was little. Really little. It was me.

I realized that what I'm really good at is helping other people with their businesses. I've always done this in one form or another, from right back in my corporate days helping companies innovate, through to advising friends on their start-ups. I may have made mistakes with my own businesses in the past, but maybe that's what gives me the ability to spot issues with other businesses. And other people seemed to agree. They started coming to me asking me to help them. Their faith in me breathed life back into my confidence, and I set up my business coaching practice.

But I still hadn't quite got it right. Happy to be back working again, and even happier to finally be out the house, I stumbled forth, squinting at the sunlight, arms outstretched, like a creature just released into the wild… straight into the one-man-band bog.

Squelch.

It was a beautiful day. I was off to meet one of my lovely new clients in a café. Obviously I had bought enough designer stationery to kit out an entire stationery fetishists' convention. Happy days!

She was a local woman with a teeny business and a tiny budget to match. Because I wasn't totally confident about what I was offering yet, and because I felt sorry for her, and because she was a friend of a friend, I'd given her a special rate. (Yes, I know, I know.)

Our coaching session went brilliantly. I was having fun and we ran hours over our allotted time. We made a big breakthrough on her business. I took notes. Lots of notes. It was late, so we decided to have some lunch. I paid. I enthusiastically promised to type up my notes and send them to her that afternoon. #boss.

After one final cappuccino, she waved me off cheerily. I felt fabulous. I knew I'd really made a difference to her life and her business.

As I wandered home slowly through the town center, my gaze wandered and so did my feet; into my favorite store, where, feeling successful and on top of the world I splashed some serious cash. In fact I splashed around $200.

Feeling like I was a total rock star, on the way home I made a mental note to send her the invoice. What had we agreed? $100 for the session.

Except, I wasn't really a rock star, was I? #notsuchabossnow

I had notes to type up. It was already time to fetch Jacob from school. Where had the day gone?! I'd spent $200 and hadn't even sent the invoice for the coaching session yet. And even when I got paid, what I'd charged wasn't even going to cover my time, let alone all the expertise I'd sent her way.

What a muppet. Everything I'd been accused of was coming true. And like a fool, I'd actually walked right into this mess.

It was all very well. I was having a great time, but I was playing at it. I'm a little embarrassed to own up to some of this, but it's important to recognize that it's easily done. Even someone who can give out great advice to others can slip up on their own path. There's a steep, slippery, slimy slope leading down into that bog.

Squelch.

When my bank statement came through that month, it was filled with all the wrong kind of zeroes. I decided it was time to make some big changes.

My reinvention process was not entirely straightforward. There was a lot of mindset trash holding me back. But then I suddenly saw the answer. It was a revelation.

The things that were scaring me the most were actually my super powers.

My little voice. That was what made me stand out.

My doubts and confidence issues. So many people feel the same way; it was a key to connecting with them.

My ambition to think big while I stayed small. It was the solution to the kind of business I should be starting.

So I started to create a completely unique brand; the brand of me. I embraced my little voice, incorporating it along with my other insecurities into my brand. I launched a business advice podcast called Little Voice Big Business.

I stopped looking locally and started thinking globally. I focused like a laser beam on my ideal clients, no matter where they lived in the world.

I put my prices up. Way, way up. I said goodbye to selling my time for money. I created products I could make money on without lifting a finger.

But I still stayed true to my goals; I didn't let my business get out of control. I didn't splash out on offices or start taking on staff or selling off equity. It was still just me.

All this—it was the bones of a little big business.

It didn't have to get physically bigger, because it already had what's needed hidden inside it. And it could be scaled so that it had massive impact.

Nowadays, my life is pretty damn lovely. I work from home, on my own and I run a successful, profitable business, often in pajamas.

It's global. I help clients all over the world; from Mauritius and America, to Sweden and New Zealand, to scale up their businesses. I have a podcast with listeners scattered all over the globe. I regularly give talks in the UK and the US.

It's big. Rather than working with one client at a time, I've created an online business academy called the Profit Pack that allows me to help female entrepreneurs worldwide to scale up and make more money.

It's flexible. Sometimes I sit at the kitchen table, sometimes I work in my tiny beautiful office and sometimes I go to a café - because I can and that's where I do my best thinking. And sometimes, don't tell anyone, but I sit on the sofa, under a blanket, with Bobby the dog keeping me warm and snuggly. Lush. My work days are short. I only work around 4 hours a day and I have time to do the school run, walk the dog, go to Pilates and boxing, and meet friends for brunch on a school day. My business is bendier than a double jointed ballerina.

It's smart. Rather than giving away chunks of my business, I hire people as and when I need them. I have a virtual team who help me with everything from tech stuff, advertising, illustration, web design, and video editing so that I can get on with helping my clients.

It's simple. Because I'm in charge and it's just me, there are no complications, no investors, no pesky partners, expensive premises or employees. My business is a serene, lean, money-making machine!

I choose to work alone. I'm not a solopreneur or a micro business; I'm a lone ranger. I like it this way. I'm flexible and free. This isn't pathetic. It's not playing small. Or any of that crap. It's about being smart and designing a business around your life. Business, and life, ends up happier that way.

I may not be a multi-millionaire, a celebrity or a business legend, (yet) but what I have done is create a business that allows me to scale. **It's little, but it gets big results.**

And these are changes you can make too, to scale your business so that it stays manageable but has big impact. And I'm going to show you how to do it too.

Are Crazy Hours and Tiny Profits Your Reality?

Is your business just you, working from home or a single desk somewhere, fitting it all in amongst your other responsibilities?

You're probably juggling a few of those responsibilities. Yes, you're dedicated to your business, but you're also dedicated to your kids, family, house, friends, pets, voluntary work, elderly relatives—all that stuff. And you might like to shower, eat and do some exercise once in a while. That doesn't leave a lot of time for you to actually run your business. It's all part of life's rich tapestry. But the fact is there's just one patchwork square for your business in the quilt of your life.

I hear you. But let me tell you, working harder is not the answer. You're already working hard. Even if you worked all day and all night, I bet you still can't see how you'd make enough money. And forget getting up at 5am, I mean there are limits, right? And that's the problem. There are simply not enough hours in the day. It's such a cliché, but you've done the math, and there literally aren't.

So, if your business is only you and you're selling your time for money, well, if there's not much time then there's not much money.

A Little Business with Big Impact

Just because your business is just you doesn't mean it has to be small impact. A tiny business can pack a major punch.

Set it up right and you can have a business that thrives and compliments your busy, multi-tasking, multi-talented life. You can go big at the same time as keeping things simple and stress-free.

So, how do you turn your small-time idea into a profit explosion? By working smarter. And I'm going to show you how.

Making Smart Changes

Every business has the potential to be bigger and to make more money. I'm going to help you get things sorted. We need to make some big changes, both to your mindset to your business strategy. A double whammy.

Maybe you need to

- adjust your target audience
- change your business model
- put up your prices
- create a sales process
- look for additional revenue streams
- automate elements of your business
- be more consistent in your marketing efforts

Making changes doesn't mean you're weak, or a failure. The definition of madness is doing the same thing again and again and expecting a different outcome. It's time to get your active wear on so you can start pivoting and turning and twisting and bending, until you find the solution.

But before we go any further, we need to get something straight.

I'm good at what I do, but I'm not a wizard. I don't ride a rainbow-colored unicorn, although I would like to. Imagine that, a lone ranger on a unicorn... but, I digress.

I know certain people would like us to believe that it's simple, this making money malarkey. That through some formula sprinkled with fairy dust, we can just click our heels and snap, the cash will rain down upon us. And yet, surprisingly, it's not quite that straightforward.

You need to do the work. I can guide you and give you useful strategies and ideas to try, but you have to actually make changes and implement things.

I'm here to help you, like I've helped hundreds of entrepreneurs before you. Together we're going to get your business sorted.

There will be no more playing small and no more limitations on what you can achieve! Together we're going to kick fear in the face and turn your tiny profits into big bucks.

Let's get started.

THE PROFIT PATH

BIG VISION
Get clear on where you're going and sort your head out

BIG PERSONALITY
Discover what makes you unique so you can stand out from the crowd

BIG LOVE
*Find your perfect people, understand what
they want and build loving relationships*

BIG PROFIT
Design your business and the way you work to make you more money!

BIG IMPACT
Crucial skills to create a consistent flow of clients

BIG
VISION

Kick Fear In The Face

I remember the first time I realised there was something a bit odd about my voice. I was fifteen, in a French lesson and we'd just got these fancy new tape machines. (I'm really ageing myself now!) You spoke into the headset and recorded your voice onto the tape so you could listen back to yourself and check your pronunciation. I loved French, despite my appalling British accent. So I happily recorded myself and then pressed play.

All I could hear was this little kid talking. Who the heck was that?

It took me a moment to realise that it was me. What the?! I sounded like I was five years old. How on earth had I not known this before? How had nobody ever mentioned this? I excused myself and hid in the loo.

I was devastated. I was a freak. From that day on I vowed to keep this little voice of mine under wraps. Since then, I've avoided letting people hear me speak. It's held me back professionally, as I hated phoning people I didn't know, leaving answer machine messages, making videos, being interviewed and public speaking. Under no circumstances would I put myself out there, exposed to potential public ridicule. If I could have communicated solely through the medium of mime, I would have done.

When my friend Emily and I set off on a mission to write a book featuring interviews with the country's most inspiring women (from Everest climbers and rock photographers, to computer scientists and famous authors) to find out how they turned their dreams of success into reality, something had to change.

It was all very well this big plan of ours, but I was scared of phoning people I didn't know. I mean, who on earth would take me seriously when I sound like I need parental supervision to use the phone. How the hell was I going to ring people up and arrange interviews with inspirational icons? We had a publisher waiting for our book and I couldn't bring myself to make the flipping phone calls.

I had a choice. No calls meant no interviews. No interviews meant no book. No book meant no deal!

In the end I just had to get on with it. And you know what? A funny thing happened. My success rate was through the roof. Whether people were so taken by the sheer brilliance of our book idea, they felt sorry for me, or thought I was doing a school project, who knows, but it seemed to work!

After a decade of hiding my voice away I realised that if only I could just push myself past the fear, great things could really happen. I haven't looked back.

It's a constant battle though. I set myself these awesome goals, and pretty much instantly, The Fear sets in. It's like a disease, and it spreads. And you may well recognise The Fear in yourself, but the worst thing is that you may not even realise you have it.

You're in the zone growing your business and single-handedly preparing for world domination. But it's there, lurking… ready to screw with your plans.

Maybe you're so busy flipping from one thing to another that you simply can't focus on the big important things you know will benefit your business. Think it's because you just don't have time? Yeah, right. You're procrastinating, because of The Fear.

So you've suddenly found yourself struck down by the lurgy when you're about to do something important, like launch a new product or give a big presentation. Chances are your sneaky subconscious has got to work putting a lid on it, in a desperate attempt to keep your greatness in an airtight Tupperware container. Why? The Fear.

Are you obsessed with making everything perfect before it sees the light of day? Stop kidding yourself that you're striving for perfection. You're avoiding taking action, dude. Because of The Fear.

Telling yourself you're keeping your prices low because you're 'attracting clients', 'building a portfolio' or 'gaining experience' before you charge properly? No - you're letting your insecurities trash your business, because… you guessed it, The Fear.

You see, it all comes down to The Fear, in the end.

You may be desperate to take off and float towards huge success and unimaginable riches, but no matter what you do, you're not getting anywhere, because you're dragging a bunch of old mindset junk behind you. Every time you surge forwards, The Fear kicks in. It keeps you safe and small, so you don't have to worry.

You don't need these doubts, fears or insecurities, but for some reason you can't let them go.

But what if you did jettison the trash and tell your fears to do one? What if you could set yourself free, so that you can stop dragging yourself down and really start to rock your business?

A Tale of Two Grandmas

I'm lucky enough to still have two grandmas. They're both just over 90 years old. They both survived the Second World War. Both of them are wonderful in their own way, but they're very different people.

Lily and Sylvie are fiercely independent women, particularly now that they have lost their husbands. Lily still insists on catering for the whole family when we visit; refusing any offer of help or gifts. And Sylvie can often be found up a ladder painting the outside of her house (not a particularly good idea, IMHO, but that's a story for another day).

It struck me recently that both my grandmas have a very different approach to life.

Lily is one hundred percent focused on making sure we, her family, are all kept safe and sound. She's not too keen on us taking risks, it worries her.

"Hey grandma, I'm off to university! And I'm going to spend a year living abroad!"

"What do you want to do that for?"

"Hey grandma, I'm starting a business."

"Oh!... What do you want to go and do that for?!"

"Hey grandma, I've decided to write a book."

"What do you want to do that for?"

You get the idea.

I do know Grandma Lily is only trying to keep me out of harm's way. She doesn't want me to take a risk unless she can be sure there's going to be a positive outcome.

Grandma Sylvie on the other hand is rather more intrepid. (Remember the ladder?) Her signature look is a Burberry trench and a Liberty's head-scarf knotted in her hair. (I swear, she's actually the original hipster.) Never a woman of great means, Grandma Sylvie has a history of blagging her way into the most glamorous high society events.

When Sylvie bumps into someone in the street, it's never some random asking for a cigarette. It's some fashion designer or wealthy foreigner who ends up inviting her to take high tea, to the royal polo or to the front row of a super luxe fashion show. Sylvie sure knows how to fake it til you make it.

It's funny how different my grandmas are. And I'm sure, even though at times it pains me to admit it, I have elements of them both in me.

When faced with change or challenge one part of me says, "What do you want to do that for?" and the other gives me a big shove and tells me to get up the ladder and get on with it.

It's up to me who I decide to listen to.

★ ★ ★ CASE STUDY: JESSICA ★ ★ ★
Jessica Andrews is a brand stylist
www.rabbitandotherstories.com

When I first started my business I had a vision of myself that was completely at odds with how other people saw me, and it showed. I knew I had skills, but I didn't think that anyone would want to pay me for them.

When you work for an employer you have a management hierarchy and company mission to work to. As an entrepreneur you have to create these yourself, and it can be very easy, working by yourself, to stop and listen to the little gremlins in your head telling you to shut up, get over yourself, and go back to working in an office, like everyone else.

Nadia helped me put my fears back in their box by encouraging me to evaluate my skills and put them together into packages that would help other small businesses. Pushing past my fears is a daily challenge. Learning to cut out the noise of well meaning family and friends has been the biggest lesson. This is the way to productivity. My fear has ceased to be the monster hiding under the bed.

Why do we get stuck in fear? It's simple really. Our brains are hardwired to keep us safe and in one place, away from the lions and monsters that could gobble us up in one slobbery mouthful.

I like to imagine that we have our very own mission control going on up there, where a team of mischievous mini mindset monkeys in boiler suits are working their little monkey butts off to keep us in the safe zone.

Picture the scene. You're about to send an invoice and the monkeys start bickering.

"Monkey control!"

"What's that she's working on?"

"I think it's an invoice."

"A what?"

"Don't make me explain—this is an emergency, you idiot"

"What does it say?"

"$5000"

"Holy crap."

"We can't do that."

"They might say no."

"They'll hate her."

"Judge her."

"It's not very seemly is it?" (That's the weird old-fashioned mini monkey)

"Let's change it."

"Best be on the safe side, eh?"

"I know... let's halve it!"

"Cools. Safe."

"Sorted."

"Phew. Panic over."

"Let's all have a nice sit down and a cup of tea shall we?"

These mini monkeys may be cute, but they're super annoying! Before you know it, you've caved and taken the safe route. Thanks for nothing, monkeys! And it doesn't end there. You're about to record a video for your audience and all hell breaks loose.

"Alert alert. Here we go again!"

"What is it?"

"She's making a video. She's turning on the camera."

"Whyyyyyy?"

"Not again!"

"Apparently it's to grow her organic reach so she can warm people up ready for her next launch. Whatever that means!"

"But what if people don't like it?"

"Or they laugh?!"

"She's put on a couple of pounds this month. People will notice."

"And look at the state of her face. Like a pizza."

"Hey, lads! It's working!"

"She's changed her mind."

"Phew. Panic over."

Every time you push yourself a little further the monkeys leap into action. You can see how much effort it takes to smack them down. But little by little they get weaker, their fur all matted and bedraggled until they're dragging themselves along the floor, barely able to reach the control desk, let alone muster the energy to have a go at you.

Clearly I have more doubts and insecurities than a teenager in the midst of an existential crisis. And yet, I've managed to write two books and grow multiple businesses. How?

Simple. The self-sabotaging efforts of those fear monkeys are no match for my arsenal of techniques designed to reset your mindset. Step off monkeys, step off!

★ ★ ★ CASE STUDY: HELEN REBELLO ★ ★ ★
Helen Rebello empowers entrepreneurs to
live and work in a way that feeds their soul
www.thetranquilpath.co.uk

I'm an accidental entrepreneur. I'm a therapist and transformational mentor first and foremost, and it was only as I went along that I realised I had a business. But I was beset by fears; I knew virtually nothing about structuring or growing a business strategically. I was nervous of being seen, of 'owning' my stuff by talking about it. I had money mindset issues, doubts about my ability to offer what I wanted to - the lot.

I reached a point where I knew the only thing limiting me was myself. I had heard an inner call to play bigger, to offer something more than myself, but in order to do so I needed to accept my limitations.

I adopted a beginners mindset, going back to basics to learn how to build a business. I changed the actions I was taking. That, in itself, started the process of believing I could play bigger and really show up as myself.

Now, I'm writing a book, I've been on stage in London sharing my story (despite a lifelong fear of public speaking), and am going to feature as a co-host/wellness expert on 12 episodes of an online TV show!

I had already identified what my underlying mission in life was - my 'why' - this has kept me going and helped me break through all the residual fears that come up as I keep pushing through new comfort zones. I keep this bigger 'why' in my mind daily - to the point where it has become so much bigger than my fears, and I can use my own skillset to help me push through.

How to Banish The Fear

Growing a business on your own isn't easy. But you're doing it! Which means that you're braver and bolder than most people. In fact, you're an entrepreneurial warrior. Sure, there are more ups and downs than a trampolining convention. But, by acknowledging them as normal, you can give yourself permission to relax and go with the flow.

Here are some techniques for taming those fears.

1. Reframe your fear

Whenever I'm about to move my business to the next level or do something new I feel a tightening in my chest. I choose to rebrand this feeling from crippling fear to adrenaline-fuelled excitement.

After all, if I didn't get all sweaty and want to puke at some point during most weeks, life would be a lot more boring, wouldn't it?

Choose to see this as the ultimate rush. Being the boss is exciting. You get to do whatever the hell you want. Yeah! You're in complete control. It's the most excitement you can have in a business setting with your clothes on.

2. Test it!

Our obsession with perfection flies in the face of reason and is seriously damaging our chances of success. In fact, if you were running a startup in Silicon Valley you'd be out on your ear.

Don't spend weeks or even longer working on something and then find that nobody wants it. It sounds completely ridiculous and yet I see this happening all the time; business owners so obsessed with making something perfect for fear of not living up to their own incredibly high standards. I'm all for high standards, but this is a form of procrastination, and it comes from a place of fear.

Instead of aiming for perfect, let's make a choice; to think of our businesses as a very tiny startup incubator. We may not refer to our office as the Mothership, have a ping pong table in every room, a dinosaur skeleton or slides between floors, but that doesn't mean we can't embrace the spirit of innovation.

Let's view everything you do as a test. Put stuff out there, see what happens and adjust as necessary. No pressure. No need for perfection. Sell ideas and then get paid to develop them.

3. Detect Procrastination

What's your fall back procrastination position? Recognise it and push through it. It's as simple as that. I know that procrastination strikes me when I'm meant to be doing admin and I magically find myself shopping for stationery and new handbags.

Can you imagine, the procrastination that took place when I decided to write this book? I mean, it's long. There are a lot of words. And although I love to write, attempting such an epic project all on my own has been daunting.

To give you an idea of the extent of the problem, I took time out of my busy writing schedule to write you a little song about it.

A LITTLE SONG ABOUT PROCRASTINATION
You're meant to be planning world domination,
But your fears turn into procrastination!
You're meant to be clearing emails
But you end up painting your nails.
That's procrastination!
You're meant to be writing that big scary talk.

Instead you take the dog for a walk.
That's procrastination!
You're meant to be following up
Instead you're washing up.
That's procrastination!
You're meant to be writing your book.
Instead you're writing a not very good song about procrastination.
That's procrastination!

4. Be wary of strange events

Alice, a member of my Profit Pack academy, shared a story recently. "I was having a good day," she said. "I was sitting in the kitchen reviewing my pricing. Even though my belly was going mad, I'd made the decision to increase my prices. And then, just as I was writing down the new figures … half of my kitchen ceiling caved in! So then I'm on my hands and knees cleaning up debris instead of getting on with my planning and updating my website with the new prices. And all I can think of is that we can't afford to have the work done right now. I'm trying not to freak out!"

Has something odd like this ever happened to you? You're about to take a big step forwards and you get sick, your computer dies, or something dramatic happens. I'm not a big one for the woo woo stuff, but honestly, WTF?!

Sometimes when we're about to do something scary, random things occur, as if the universe is trying to sabotage our efforts so that we'll give it up and stay firmly slumped on the sofa. Or maybe it's just that our subconscious is looking for that big excuse not to get on and do what we need to.

In the face of collapsing ceilings and broken down cars, a weaker person would throw in the towel and go get a job. But you're made of stronger stuff. So if you're hit by a random piece of ceiling, simply clean up the mess, dust yourself off and get on with building your empire.

5. Pick a perk
Every time you kick fear in the face, give yourself a prize. You deserve it! Remember how motivating it used to feel to get a bonus or an award when you had a job? Well, you're the boss now, which means you're in charge, so don't forget.

6. Positive words
I love a good mantra. I like to wear a bangle with my favorite phrase and it gives me confidence. I realise that sounds ridiculous, but if it works, why the heck not? When I'm struggling I check my wrist, see these positive words and press on. Take that monkeys!

You got this!
I can and I will.
She believed she could, so she did.

7. Get help
Hiring a business coach was the best thing I ever did. When I'm struggling with the monkeys, she helps me get to the root of the problem so I can press on. Sometimes, trying to bat those monkeys away all on your own is too hard. That's when you know it's time to bring in the big guns. You may be on your own, but you don't have to do it alone.

8. Just flippin' do it
You're committed to this business of yours. It has to happen. Nobody else can do it for you. So, scared or not, it's time to crack on, one little step at a time. I've come to realise that my fear will never subside. It's in my

nature to be filled to the brim with doubts and insecurities apparently. And that's OK. But, now I know what's going on and I can wave to the monkeys, acknowledge the fear and then press on regardless.

★ ★ ★ CASE STUDY: SALLY ★ ★ ★
Sally Chamness is a massage therapist
www.dynamicbodywork.co.uk

When I first took over my business, relationships with the previous owner were volatile and my confidence in my abilities were rock bottom. Every day was a struggle to continue, and I felt like one wrong step and I would have given up and folded the business right there and then.

Fear has been my biggest hurdle. The process of acquiring the businesses had left me so beaten I felt like I had already failed. I didn't want to risk failure again. I could hear the voice of the previous owner in my head every time I tried to come up with something new, or something that I felt was new or exciting.

I didn't believe I was capable of making it a success. I felt like a fraud. I had been told during the transition phase that everything I was trying to do to make the business work was wrong. I doubted every idea I had.

I was having a crisis of faith about a course I had scheduled that involved an international presenter when Nadia got involved. She showed me how to take action steps to do something that terrified me, and it left me feeling brave and empowered.

I've now planned an amazing return to the spotlight and launched with a BANG. I've developed the confidence to put myself out there and market the business with authority.

★ ★ ★

Just focus!

Today I'm writing. I've set aside a big chunk of time to give this chapter my undivided attention.

But, I'm also running a Facebook ad campaign and I've become obsessed with checking my stats and conversions. Like a compulsive checker nutter. What am I doing? I'm messaging the people on my team to see who has the most sign-ups. We're in a Facebook chat group. Comparing numbers. Back and forth, back and forth.

I'm meant to be focusing on this chapter. A chapter about focus. What am I doing?!

I'll just get back to it. Oh wait a minute, what was that thing I was meant to remember? Oh yeah, I need to pay for Jacob's school dinners. And make sure I pay that invoice. I'll just dig that email out while I'm here. Hmm... so many emails. Maybe I'll delete a few. Oooh, look, a discount code for the Gap. I'll just have a little browse. I may as well check up on my Twitter. And take some aspirational photos of my desk and coffee for Insta. And maybe I'll make some funny photos on Snapchat, of me looking like a gangsta kitten or a sexy rabbit.

An hour later and I still haven't read any of my emails, or paid that invoice. I'm all over the place. Chopping and changing. Jumping from one thing to the next, like I'm doing parkour.

And as for writing this chapter. Not a chance.

I'll just make a coffee. I've only got one coffee pod left, so I pop online and order some more. Wow. They're expensive aren't they? Oooh, look mince pie flavour coffee. I wonder what that's like. Hmm... not sure. Might be a bit sickly. I'll stick with the normal ones. Closed systems, eh– it's genius really, the way they hook you into buying their pods for the rest of your life.

Friends is on TV. I know I'm probably the only person who still watches it. I don't have any excuse or explanation really, but it's my guilty work-from-home pleasure. Before I know it, the whole day is gone and it's time for me to go pick up Jacob from school. Doh.

Frankly, it's a miracle I've even got a business. Let alone one that makes money!

Too Many Tabs Open

There are so many different things we could be doing to grow our businesses, but our lives are so busy it's astonishing we can function at all. We have too many tabs open, literally, as well as in our lives, and in our businesses and our brains.

But, rather than making a plan and tackling them in order of priority, we've turned multi-tasking into an extreme sport.

I'm a master at watching TV, reading the paper on my iPad, listening to music, talking on the phone, making dinner and painting my nails, all at the same time. Admittedly, I'm not doing a great job at any of those things, but I feel like I'm winning at life when I'm doing it.

And the problem is, working like this is so utterly unproductive. Jumping from one tab to the next as each new thought occurs to you means you're left with a whole bunch of uncompleted tasks.

I literally have to force myself to write a note for later, rather than immediately leap to open a new tab and get sucked down the next rabbit hole.

We're all becoming champion flitters. At the Flitters Olympics I'd be a real contender! Imagine the medal ceremony, we'd all be on our phones, writing our shopping lists, tweeting, taking silly photos on Snapchat, having sex, all at the same time.

Social media is a big culprit when it comes to distracting us. The pinging, it's both highly irritating and highly addictive. Facebook messages, emails, Twitter notifications, Instagram hearts, Whatsapp messages. Jeez. Our attention spans have been reduced to gnat-like proportions.

Remember when you had to look stuff up in encyclopaedia to find the answers, or actually get off our butts and go to the library. It's mad when you think about it. That wasn't even very long ago! Now all the data, information and stuff is at our fingertips, or we can just ask Alexa, it's no wonder that we feel like we're drowning.

Shiny Object Syndrome

Marketers have infiltrated our minds. As we go about our business on multiple platforms, there are ads everywhere, woven into every stream and sidebar; all selling us a shinier, more fabulous life and business.

You can't even drool over other people's perfectly stylish dinner plates of avocado smush on Instagram without finding yourself purchasing some ropey-looking tea that promises to obliterate 40lbs of flab in just 48 hours.

And if you weren't tempted the first time, the ad will stalk you, like a whole bunch of creepy old men, offering you sweets and puppies, until you finally cave and succumb to their promises.

You only logged on to check those emails remember, and before you know it, you've bought another online program promising you the earth. You were wandering around the internet aimlessly, and suddenly you've parted with thousands of dollars! How did that happen?

And with the rise of affiliate marketing people we admire unite in their endorsement of each others' highly persuasive programs, solutions and formulae to help us get thinner, be more attractive and make more money in our businesses.

For a moment there's a rush of dopamine as you feel that you may finally have found the solution to all your ills. And then a bunch of emails arrive in your inbox. The inbox you haven't even checked yet. Ugh. Not feeling quite so good now are you?

Even the most resilient, bootstrapping entrepreneur can succumb to these persuasive tactics. I've seen people jump from one solution to the next in the hope of growing their businesses, each time believing that this next thing will be the key to their success. I've even signed up for some of this stuff myself, and more often than not, it's been utterly underwhelming.

Obviously, I'm all about helping people like you to grow their businesses. But my ambition for you is that you grow your business and make more money in the process, not bankrupt yourself, sell your car, or take out a second mortgage! If the only thing you buy in order to do that is this book, then that's wonderful.

Before you sign up for anything else, take a moment to think it through, away from the pressure of any sleazy sales tactics. Check out the reviews. Ask people who've done it before and get their honest opinions. Run the numbers and make sure you can really afford it. Do not, under any circumstances go into debt, in order to fund your business. Get a job if you need to but do not go into debt! Be sure that it really delivers what you need and that it's a top priority right now for you and your business.

Crushing Overwhelm

From where I'm sitting, on the front row of the catwalk that is business life, overwhelm is definitely the new black. It's taken over as the entrepreneurial state of mind. You know it.

You wake up, and think to yourself, what am I going to do today to grow the heck out of my business? Bosh. And there it is. Overwhelm sets in, like a big octopus sitting on your head, with slimy tentacles that wrap themselves around you, squishing your innards and making you feel anxious and more than a little panicky. There's so much to do that you're not sure where to focus. All your positivity has vanished.

You're meant to be running a successful business, #likeaboss. But this overwhelm, sucks the life and energy out of you. It makes you feel like a complete failure.

But you're not a failure. Running a business all on your own is tough. Really tough. Did I mention it's tough?

When you have a job you could probably often just get on with doing what you're told. That has its obvious drawbacks, particularly if you have an issue with authority, like I do, but on the other hand, it kinda takes the pressure off, doesn't it?

But when you work alone it's hard to stay focussed. Seeing the bigger picture becomes near impossible when you're focusing on getting through each day, one at a time. There's a reason why people hire consultants and coaches. It's incredibly difficult to get a clear and objective sense of what to do in your business when you're stuck in it.

Something has to change. It's time to smash overwhelm into smithereens, because this situation right now, this octopus feeling of struggling under lots of different ideas and things you could be doing, sure as hell isn't helping you grow your business.

Be a Specialist

In my spare time I like doing all kinds of different things. I like boxing, horses, sculpture, watching Jacob play football and sometimes even playing a bit myself, French cinema watching Big Bang Theory. I'm multifaceted; multi-passionate; me.

I may often be tempted, but I don't run a business for each of these things. (I admit I did have a blog called French Film Club for a while, but 187 film reviews later, I soon got fed up with that, convinced I'd never watch another French film again.)

Just because you are passionate about something doesn't mean you need to turn it into a business. Specialising in one thing is good!

My mother and I have been "discussing" this issue for a while now. She would like my son Jacob to have a range of interests. Not that she has any say in the matter, but she wants him to be a rounded individual with lots of hobbies. Sounds good in theory, but he has other ideas. Of course he does! He's one feisty little person.

Jacob is 100% focused on football. He lives and breathes soccer. It's everything to him. And you know what, he's become really rather good at it. He's worked his socks off over the years—in fact he's worked so hard that those sweaty socks could pretty much walk themselves into the washing machine. I'm incredibly proud of his dedication actually. He's not the biggest or the strongest on his team, but he's created a name for himself as a genius at passing the ball, nicknamed One-Touch Jacob.

As I pointed out to my mother, she too is a specialist. My mom is an inventor and has spent the past 20 years focusing like an obsessive compulsive laser on a special valve that has enabled her to create two mind-blowing products. If she has been a generalist with a range of interests she'd still be sitting at home brainstorming. Ha, in your face, mom!

Do one thing, and do it brilliantly. Everything else can wait.

★ ★ ★ CASE STUDY: ERIN FOGGOA ★ ★ ★
Erin Foggoa is an artist with a unique steampunk style
www.erinfoggoacreative.com

My business was spread out so far that I could barely breathe! I was catering to every single person who would throw money at me and it was exhausting. I love what I do for a living - I mean; I get to make art! But, I was not loving my income; I was working seven days a week and making nothing.

I was hiding behind a pseudonym when I found Nadia, and I really wasn't being me. As soon as she'd assessed my business, Nadia told me to stop hiding. Soon my business went from three different pseudonyms to MY NAME! It's my art, I am signing it, and it is all about me. I am sharing my passion, so it can't be from behind a veil.

Now, I am back in love with my business. I am learning a work-play balance that I just did not have before. This last month I finally embraced the real passion for my business. I decided to go for broke and just ASK the companies I want to work with to join forces with me, and I am overwhelmed by the YES response.

I got the go ahead from two major animal rescue projects, and I am going to be drawing their animals, making money for their rescues and also telling my stories, and helping share these animals with the world. I am using my talent to make positive change, there is nothing quite like that.

I moved into my new studio a year ago this week, I am hiring a marketing team next month and I am taking HUGE leaps and risks this year, massive. I am not sure if I could've done it, or how many more years I could've plodded along, if it weren't for the push from Nadia and my fellow Profit Packers.

Park It

I have an affliction. I have ideas oozing out of every orifice. I've got a bad case of idea-rrhea! And it's catching.

I love having ideas. I'm pretty good at it too. In fact, I used to get paid to have ideas. But just because they're spewing forth, doesn't mean I need to act on them all. If your brain is bubbling away with tiny baby ideas vying for your attention, it's really hard to focus on growing your business.

I get that you don't want to lose them, or forget them. But you have to get them out of your head and onto paper. The solution is simple. You just need to write them down in a notebook and keep them somewhere safe for a rainy day when you need them. You definitely don't need them pinging around your brain like a pinball machine.

If you don't do this, there's a clear and present danger that you'll end up muddying what you're doing as these sly little critters infiltrate your work. Without you even noticing they'll be confusing everything and everyone your business comes into contact with. Eventually you'll have created something so convoluted that even Miss Marple wouldn't be able to work it out.

Spell It Out

I was recently asked to review a website for a client. I started with the home page, but no matter how many times I read it through I couldn't work out what the business was about. I moved to the About page. Still no idea. Not a sausage. Perhaps I had brain fog? I drank some coffee. Did some star jumps. Took the dog for a walk. And still, for the life of me, I couldn't work out what it was all about!

This website was like a pair of jeans that had been upcycled, patched up, embellished. It had lost all sense of what it once was, and frankly had become a complete dog's dinner. It was clear it had been fiddled with so many times, as the focus of the business had shifted from side to side, that it had ended up completely incoherent.

And faced with this mess, potential clients were likely to be just walking away.

Be brave enough to focus. Make it simple for your clients. Tell them what you do, clearly and concisely. Be the 'Facebook ads girl'; the 'stylist for moms who love vintage'; the 'fitness instructor for pastry chefs'. Focus on one thing. Be brilliant at that one thing. Become famous for it. Be bright and bold, not some sludgy shade of brown. Make it clear. Super clear.

Money-Making Activities

Think about successful people in your field. Do they do 95 different things for all kinds of different people? I'm going to hazard a guess and say, no! They do less, a lot less. But they do it really well.

Stop trying to do all the things and focus on what works best.

You know the 80/20 rule, or Pareto's Principle, that explains why you only ever wear the same couple of pairs of shoes, even though your cupboard is rammed to the rafters? That Pareto dude is on the money when it comes to use running our businesses too. 20% of what you're doing right now creates 80% of your results and revenue.

Have a think about your business and see if that rings true. I bet there's a whole glut of things you're doing right now that get you precisely nowhere. These things are a total waste of time.

Look at your numbers and see where the cashola is coming from and then take a moment to declutter. Just imagine how much more profitable and effective you'll be if you are just doing the things that work. Being busy and scattered is not a sign of success. Being busy is not big or clever. Running a business that makes money is!

Roxanne the stylist came to me with 23 different services. Her website was so confusing. There were services layered upon other services. And multiple packages within each layer. Brain explosion. I was fairly sure her clients just wanted to sort out a new look, they didn't expect to get a migraine looking at her site! On further examination, it turned out that people tended to email her directly and ask for one of just three packages; the wardrobe edit, the colour analysis and the style session. So, guess what I suggested. See if you can. Go on, have a go! Whoa. Radical. Did she lose clients? Nope. She got more enquiries. I must be a genius. Ha ha!

Take a step back from all the stuff. What is it that really leads to results in your business?

Do you know that if you give a talk you get loads of new clients? If you run Facebook ads? Or you do some sales calls? Identify your money-making activities and do more of them. Stop doing the things that don't work. Focus on the thing or things that make money. And do more of that. Hit it hard!

Get a Plan, Man

I used to just kind of drift along in my business with a general sense that I knew roughly where I was going. It was a bit like my approach to navigating on a long journey. (The one that has led to my husband nearly divorcing me on more than one occasion) Gazing out the window and spotting horses and pretty houses, isn't ideal as you zoom past the motorway exit. (But, did you see, that thatched cottage? So cute!) But the thing is, there's a lot of potential for detours, getting lost and taking the scenic route accidentally on purpose. I'm a freestyler, I'm creative, don't tie me down, man.

I soon realised that if you actually want to grow your business and make money, you need to get a grip, set some goals and make a plan.

There's nothing fancy or techy about it. It's important to know where you're heading in your business. If you have a goal you can work out what you need to do to achieve it. Without a plan, you're just a penniless drifter.

On the days when I wake up feeling lost or overwhelmed by my business I know I just need to check my plan and do what it says. Having a plan means you'll never again wonder what on earth you need to do next in your business.

Being busy is bull. Endless to-do lists that are not based on a strategy just keep you busy. They don't get you closer to achieving your goals.

All good plans start with a goal. If your goal is to win five new clients this month, your plan should cover the steps to achieving this.

Now, instead of just plodding along with what you're doing, identify what is actually going to take you towards the goal, in the most effective way possible.

You don't need to spend days and days planning. An hour or so every couple of weeks will keep you on track. So there's no excuse. And who knows, you might find you even enjoy it. There's a whole super geeky planning scene out there, with people who plan, for fun. There are stickers. Don't judge me, but I kinda love it. There's something very satisfying about being organised and having everything all laid out nicely. It's therapeutic. And did I mention the stickers?

If you don't yet have a plan, all you need to do is set a goal for say the next 90 days. Break it down into key tasks and then break those down into smaller tasks. Don't keep adding more things to the list. Do what you need to do. It's simple!

★ ★ ★ CASE STUDY: ANNE ★ ★ ★
**Anne Page provides inspiration,
products and tips for speech therapists
www.beautifulspeechlife.com**

I was plodding along. I was working full-time while trying to get my business off the ground, getting pulled in so many different directions. I was dropping the ball with my family, forgetting important occasions. I was doing all this work and just breaking even. What?! Was this just a very expensive and time-consuming hobby?

The trouble was, I was vague with my goals and didn't have a clear direction. I spent a lot of money on shiny new courses because I felt they held some knowledge I was missing out on.

But since I've worked to focus on what is most important in moving my business forward, I can recognize when I'm doing that easy, busy work to distract myself from what is really going to bring in some dollars. I have a really clear plan now.

In seven months I've tripled my email subscribers. I'm automating processes and working smarter with really substantial results. I'm believing that I really can do this, it's not just something that happens to "other people." The momentum is spreading out in all areas: sales, inquiries, social media engagement and opportunities. My sales are increasing and I'm building a paid course and a membership site. I have a clear picture of where I'm going, with the flexibility to detour as the path unfolds.

Good Vibes Only

It's Challenging, This Business of Business

Running a business by yourself is a unique challenge. I love working alone and being in charge of everything, but the life of a lone ranger can mess with your mind. You're dealing with the highs and lows of running a business all by yourself. It's up to you to stay positive, motivated and upbeat and to press on through your fears—even when you'd rather curl up in a ball and hide. There are no teammates to cheer you on or give you a hand. There is no boss chasing you up or setting you deadlines or incentivizing you. It's just you, blazing a trail and fighting your fears all by your freakin' self.

And that's why positivity is so important. Having the ability to stay positive and upbeat, no matter what, often means the difference between success and failure.

★ ★ ★ CASE STUDY: JULIE CORNISH ★ ★ ★
Julie Cornish is a marketing strategist
www.juliecornish.com

"Can I become a successful entrepreneur after the age of 40? Was it wise to leave a six-figure salary, full benefits and a pension plan to start my own business? Can I really do this?"

The mind chatter and second-guessing were constant. I was terrified of starting my business, sending out my first email when my list didn't even have 100 people on it. My first attempt to host a live broadcast on a webinar failed miserably as I pressed the wrong button and my entire platform shut down.

I remember sweating profusely and I may have shed a few tears, but it didn't stop me from trying again. My determination paid off. My second webinar generated over 600 views!

What I've learned since then, and what has helped me attract clients, is embracing my power and trusting myself 100%. Allowing myself to be fully and authentically me, by building a business that reflects who I am; someone who is strategic and knowledgeable.

Making money online and having a thriving business does not need to be difficult or take time. All it takes is the right strategy, the right mindset and an unwavering commitment to making it happen.

The Power of Positivity

Positivity is incredibly powerful. We're not talking about blind optimism here, the kind where you walk around with a freaky fixed smile on your face like you've just been indoctrinated into some dodgy cult. Nor does positivity mean you're blindly wandering into situations without paying the slightest bit of notice to the risks.

This is about being a smart combo of realistic and positive at the same time. It's nothing to do with wearing rose-tinted glasses and wafting around like a hippy who's had too many magic mushrooms.

I'm talking about the kind of gritty positivity that will enable you to pick yourself up, day after day, setback after setback and keep on trying until you get to where you want to be. It's choosing to focus on the positive side of things and to squish the negativity before it has a chance to pop up; like a game of whack the rat. I reckon positivity is closely linked with grit, determination and resilience. It's about getting your game face on when things aren't panning out as anticipated. And just getting on with it.

I know it's hard to always feel upbeat. We are only human after all. Sometimes I feel a little under the weather or just really exhausted, and perhaps cracking on is the last thing I really want to do. But you can't just not do it. Not when your business is you. If you collapse into a crushed heap of self-pity your business will do the same.

Presenting a positive sunny outlook to the rest of the world is essential. Even if you are down in the dumps feeling sorry for yourself, or feeling desperate because business isn't going the way you want it to. You have to stay positive, because positivity attracts positivity.

If you are buzzing with excitement and energy for what you are doing, then other people will be drawn to you. They will want to hang out with you. They will want to work with you. Your charisma will be catching!

Don't be a Negative Nelly

If you choose to indulge in the negative and you're all like, "I can't do it, business sucks, its really difficult and I'm just so overwhelmed," people will run a mile. If you walk around feeling sorry for yourself, people are going to give you a very wide berth indeed. I promise you. You want to be attracting people with your magnetic personality, not repelling them with an impenetrable force field.

Your business might be amazing. You might have the most splendid product. A stunning brand. And be incredibly talented at what you do. But, if you've had a positivity bypass, there will be no saving you. No matter what you do, no matter how hard you work, you'll never attract clients. If you radiate negative vibes, you will destroy your business.

And that's why I'm all about the good vibes, man.

★ ★ ★ CASE STUDY: EMILY ★ ★ ★
Emily McManama is a women's empowerment life coach
www.emcommunitycoachingllc.com

In 2015, I was diagnosed with late stage three breast cancer and given a 50/50 chance of survival. I was 25.

The next year was a blur of chemotherapy, radiation, a bilateral mastectomy, blood clots, a hysterectomy, and too many surgeries to mention... but I survived.

Surviving made me realize how important it is to live your passion each day and this business became my passion. But planning a business was scary. Aside from my health issues, there were so many toxic influences in my life, telling me to play safe, go small and don't expect too much. But the heart and the passion were there, and I learned to take the strength that got me through cancer treatment and build my business on that.

Positivity has been so important for me. I remember this one time I realised I'd missed a huge opportunity. I had messed up a webpage; 5,000 views and not one person had signed up. It was easy to get discouraged. I realized that my attitude was impacting future clients. No one wants to get help from someone who is down and negative!

Pursuing a business that empowers others is empowering me. I feel more driven and each day is an exciting opportunity to see what my coaching community can accomplish. Life is too short to not reach out and pursue the life you want.

★ ★ ★

This is Not Fakery

Let me get something straight. I don't want you to lie and pretend that you're living a charmed life, like an Instagram icon.

This isn't about making out like everything is perfect, that nothing is ever tricky. You're not an eternally perky robot.

I'm a positive person, but I'm real. I don't run my business wearing a string bikini. I don't do downward dogs in a pair of hot pants while I'm writing this. I'm not gonna lie.

I'm not going to pretend anything. Least of all that running a business is easy. And that it's one laugh after another.

Instead I'm going to be real and honest and open, but I choose to focus on the positive side of things.

★ ★ ★ CASE STUDY: EVI ★ ★ ★
Evi Kathrepti is a productivity life coach
www.facebook.com/whatthehealthishappening

Looking back in my working life I realised that no matter what I did, one thing stayed constant, my approach. I always worked with people, supported them, advanced them, listened to them, empathised with them. I was a natural coach, a trainer, a teacher, a mentor. Once I realised that, I knew what my business and my future looked like.

Success is all about mindset! I had to let go of the small to look for the one thing that would make me feel that I am contributing to the world on a big scale.

Connecting with my "why" keeps me positive, because I know it is not only me I will be letting down if I do not succeed. I also surround myself with motivational cues and I do one thing every day towards the development of the business. Every day I feel like I conqueror something new and this motivates me to take the next step and persevere.

Comeback queen

Things do go wrong, but it's how you deal with it that matters. You might lose a file. A client says no. You send an email and people unsubscribe. You put a deal out and no one goes for it. But, you're not going to give up!

You're going to put a smile on your face and present a positive and energized version of you to the world and people are going to believe that everything is going fine. You're going to continue taking action. And just press on.

I don't want to hear that you have given up because things go to difficult. That you couldn't face it. That your first bash at running a business was not a blinding success and therefore you decided to go back to work. Nonsense!

When business is not going brilliantly, you don't just jack it all in. You know when to pivot and make changes. You don't get down in the dumps and feel sorry for yourself and get all moany.

I am not having it! If one more person tells me they made a Facebook ad and nobody clicked on it, so they're going to jack it all in… I think I'll scream! If it doesn't work, change the ads!

Nobody puts something out there once and expects it to work first time around. It never happens. There are always going to be improvements you could make to increase your impact.

And let's say something does go wrong. You can't have a tantrum. (Well, maybe just a small one.) You've gotta crack on and get it done.

★ ★ ★ CASE STUDY: MARIE ★ ★ ★
Marie Hernandez is an empowerment coach
www. love-creates-miracles.com

I found myself homeless, jobless, and in a foreign country at 50, forced to start my life over in a way I hadn't planned. I was freaking terrified. I had all the typical thoughts of resentment, anger; feelings of failure, loss, and betrayal a person faces when a sudden and unexpected life-changing event overtakes them.

At first I curled up, pulled the covers over my head, and didn't want to face reality. If I didn't acknowledge it, it wasn't real, right?

I had the fear. The fear of being alone, of not being good enough, of being too old. These self-defeating beliefs had me stuck.

I spent a month in bed. Then one day I swung my legs over the side and said, "Enough is enough!" I stood up, grabbed a pad of paper, went for a walk, filled my lungs with fresh air, and found a place to sit and really think about what I wanted my life to be.

The burning question was, what did I want? What direction did I want my life to head in? Since travel has always been my passion, and I had already established a good online following, I realized that this was my path.

Once I took back the responsibility for my own happiness, I was able to take on life on my own terms. Things changed for me after that. I was able to move forward and work towards the life I wanted.

Jump ahead to present day, here I am working, writing, and falling in love with myself. I'm growing my coaching business so I can spread my message of empowerment to other women who have suffered pain and loss. Am I finished discovering who I am and what I want? Hell no! But the journey is the best part, isn't it?

Positivity Planning Tips

1. Smile

All this motivation and positivity has to come from you; from somewhere inside you. And not everyone has it. If it doesn't come naturally to you, that's OK. It's time to drink you some positivitea and put a big toothy grin on your face. It's as simple as that. Like lunges, the more you practice the easier it will get.

2. Spread positive vibes

Try putting something positive out into the world on the internet each day. I don't mean boasting about how wondrously successful you are - you don't want to make people retch. Instead, share a good thing you did or that happened to you that day. It could be a great meeting you had, or an inspiring podcast you discovered. Your words and images will lift others up and good things will start to whirl around you, like the smell of cinnamon buns, nom nom!

3. Celebrate your wins

Take a moment each week to celebrate your wins, no matter how big or small. We tend to be in such a rush, zooming from one thing to the next that we can forget the good things that have happened. Focusing on the good stuff in your life and your business successes will help you create more of the good stuff.

4. Be kind to yourself

Look after yourself and your business will look after itself. If you've come down with a migraine because you've pulled another all-nighter, you've hustled to the bone, and you can't remember the last time you ate something that didn't come out of a packet, your business is going to suffer. This happens all the time! It's not a competition to see who can work the hardest. You're not a machine. So be kind to yourself. Get some rest. Eat good food. Get some exercise. Go see your friends. Your business will thank you for it.

5. Let it out

Like flatulence, it's not good for you to hold negative stuff in. It will come out eventually! I'm pretty sure it will start to ooze out of some very strange places at very strange times if you're not careful. It's OK to feel this stuff. If you're sad or upset, that's OK. Let it out. Have a cry. Stomp around. Shout out the window. Call your friends. Whatever you need to do, so that you feel better and are ready to move on.

6. Ditch the drama

It's so easy to get sucked into other people's drama. You're scrolling through your Facebook feed and suddenly you're drawn into someone's angry rant about goodness knows what. There are literally hundreds of comments. People are wading in left right and center. It's all kicking off. You read through all the comments and you're about to get involved. Don't! I know how tempting it is to speak your truth or wind people up, just for fun. But I need you to focus on growing your business not spending hours justifying your comments to a bunch of nutters. Drama has a habit of following you around like a bad smell. Avoid, avoid.

7. Let it go

When something crappy happens, acknowledge it and then let it go. Try to not to fixate and obsess about it. I'm not always the best at this! Just ask my family, he he. It takes practice. At the time it can feel like the end of the world, but often it's such a tiny little thing and tomorrow it won't matter at all. When you let it go, you'll be able to make space for fresh new positive things.

8. Shake it off

When I'm feeling down in the dumps, like nothing is working out, I get out the house. Change of scene. I walk the dog or I go sit in a café and listen to some silly pop music. Or if it's really bad, I go boxing and punch a man called Brian. Poor Brian. The stuff that man knows about me.

9. Pick positive people

Surround yourself with people who are going to boost you. Not drag you down. If you have friends who doubt you. Or moan a lot. Or question your judgment. Or make you question yourself or knock your confidence. Don't hang out with them. Surround yourself instead with people who get you. Who believe in you. I'm not saying you want an entourage of people who are going to suck up to you and agree with everything you say, but having people around you who get what you're trying to do is super useful.

10. Tune in

Music has magic powers. If you need to up your positivity, listen to some uplifting music and let it soothe your soul. Or just dance around like a loon. Whatever you need to do to get your vibe flying high.

BIG
PERSONALITY

Do 'You'

"Y ou need to leave your personality at home," my boss said. "I think it will be best for the business if you have a Work Nadia and a Home Nadia."

She actually said that! I'm not even making this up. Maybe she thought she was just finding a kind way to tell me to stop mucking about at work, but actually it was a lot more sinister than that.

She didn't want me, if me was the way me actually was. She only wanted the bit of me that was more like other people; probably the bit that behaved and did as I was told, I imagine.

The more I think about it now, the more outrageous it is. I know I was a bit of a pain and I did used struggle to conform at work, but surely it must be possible to be yourself and still be professional?

If this conversation was taking place now, I'd probably just walk straight out of the door. But in 2002, at my first ever marketing job, working for a boss who makes Meryl Streep in Devil Wears Prada look like a big ole softie, I wasn't sure what to make of her orders. I was fairly sure splitting my brain in two like a watermelon would lead to some kind of mental health issue, and besides, what was so wrong with me that I could only bring half my watermelon to work?

Unable to have a sensible grown up discussion with her (because frankly she scared the living daylights out of me), I agreed meekly and took my frustrations out on her cups of tea. I won't go into details, but, suffice to say, I couldn't quite leave the mischievous bit of me at home.

Building the Brand of You

As an entrepreneur, we get to be ourselves and embrace who we are. Finally, we're free to be fully authentic, honest, open and true to ourselves. And there's nothing easier and more natural than being yourself. Being real is so much easier than having a personality-lobotomy, going full fake, and simulating someone else.

The beauty of being yourself is that nobody can easily copy you. Like Carly Simon said, nobody does it quite the way you do.

Big powerful brands are desperate to build real relationships and create emotional electricity with their customers. They spend millions creating this calculated connection by latching on to their customers' emotions, desires and unmet needs.

The good news is that as an actual human being who is running a little big business, you have it a whole lot easier. You don't need to spend millions on focus groups or ad agencies to get to build this kind of relationship. All you need to do is be yourself.

It's the nature of being a lone ranger, that you and your business are intertwined. People are buying into you when they work with your business. They're hiring you. Which is why it makes sense for you to own who you are.

It may seem weird at first to get this personal, after all, this is business. But people buy from people. And you are your business. Nobody has experienced the things you have. Nobody is quite like you.

There are lots of reasons why embracing your personality is going to help you make more money.

Firstly, if you're being yourself, you're unique. And when you're unique, your potential clients are less likely to compare you to others. Their decision to hire you is an emotional one, because your message resonates with them, rather than a sensible pricing decision.

Embracing your personality makes it easier to attract your ideal clients. Your stories, experiences and your vibe will draw people to you and they'll sense that you are the best person to help them.

Your work will flow more easily, because it's more fun when you're being yourself. It will be easier to relate to your clients because they'll be like you. It'll be easier to know what to say to people because you'll be talking in your own voice.

Not everyone will love you. But that's OK. They can simply jog on. Instead you can focus your energy and attention on attracting your kind of people and turning them into superfans.

There are so many reasons why doing you is the way to go. So, why aren't you doing it already?

Clone Wars

Embracing who you are can be scary. Our doubts and fears and insecurities creep in and we end up holding back, not daring to be different. We feel vulnerable and exposed because we're afraid that people will judge us or even laugh at us.

It happened to me. And I see it happening to my clients too. When you're running a service-based business it feels like you're selling yourself, and that means opening yourself up to judgement and criticism. It can be paralysing.

Rather than being honest with ourselves, we look around us at everyone else and see what they're doing. Our eyes are drawn to people who are doing well, who are rocking it. Comparisonitis sets in. You want what she's got. You feel like you'll never be as good as that, or as successful or as good-looking. You look at how she's doing it, everything from her products, to her style of photography, her branding, everything. You get sucked in and you try to be more like her.

In doing so, you risk becoming a clone. You're slipping into the minion trap. This is not helpful. It's a waste of energy and is completely exhausting. You deserve more than this.

Your clients will see through it. Something will feel off for them, they'll feel uneasy, but they won't know why. Trying to be like someone else can bump off your business. Put your blinkers on and stop looking outside yourself for the answers.

★ ★ ★ CASE STUDY: MARISA MOODY ★ ★ ★
Marisa Moody, personal trainer and health coach
www.motivatedmovementpt.com

I used to worry that I didn't know as much as other personal trainers, that I didn't have the same education, training or knowledge. I couldn't help comparing the size of my list and social media following and obsessing that they were a lot bigger than me!

I used to feel insecure about how I was going to stand out in the crowded health and fitness market. I had no idea what made me different.

But when I thought about it, I realized that my individuality is what sets me apart. I am unique because of my story and my history. Nobody else has done what I've done, the way I've done it. I have struggled with weight loss, just like others. I still love cake and chocolate and wine, but now I also love hitting the gym, lifting weights and going for a run. I think my realness is what people want to connect with and I just need to stick to who I am.

It's been tough, but I've started owning it! I do know what I'm talking about, I have a lot of experience, and many clients achieve great results.

Push the self doubt aside, believe in yourself, and do it!

Will It Work for My Business?

You might be thinking that this won't work for you, because your business is somehow different. Maybe your business is super-sensible but you … not so much? If you're providing something very professional, can you still put your personality into it? Of course you can! This works for any kind of business, and here's why.

Let's say I was going to start a bookkeeping business, I would talk start by telling my story and talk about how I got into boxing and discovered the rebel within. I'd be the rebel book-keeper on a mission to bash your business into shape. I'd share how, although I'm super quiet, rather middle aged and not very strong, I discovered a savage side to myself! I could bring my style and my vibe to this business, and it would rock.

People hire people. They connect to stories and characters, and if you give them both then even something as apparently serious as a bookkeeping business will stand out. They also sense truth and can sniff out fakery, so if you're pretending you run a massive corporation when really it's just you at home in your kitchen, there's going to be a disconnect between you and potential customers. Tell your actual story and they'll trust you.

The key to putting yourself into your brand is to do it professionally. You'll need to ensure that everything you create is of a very high quality;

for example, get your copy proof read, and your videos professionally edited and have a proper photo-shoot….

Own It

I used to hide away. I was a brilliant at creating a brand and then hiding right behind it. I didn't even realise I was doing it. But that means I can spot when you're doing it!

Let me tell you the signs. You create a website but you decide not to have an About page, because no one wants to know about you, right? You post on social media using the royal 'we', when in fact there's just you. You decide people are right, you should make a video, but you sure as hell aren't going to be in it!

It was happening to Beverley when I met her. Beverly is a hypnotherapist. In real life she's a hoot. Really funny and a joy to be around. But her business was really staid. It was hard to put your finger on it, but there was a disconnect. The videos she released used animation instead of featuring her. Her webinars and video trainings were delivered by an actor's voice. Her social media posts looked like they'd been churned out by a huge corporation. It made it really hard for people to bond with her, like her, trust her, and therefore to hire her. By trying to be all serious and businessy, she was holding her real self and her business back. And yet, get her down the pub and she's hilarious!

I worked with Beverly to create a more personal brand. Now she's telling her story from the heart in a completely authentic way. She's appearing in her videos even though at first she was scared, and working on becoming more intuitive in the way she talks to her people. Rather than pretending to be a faceless corporation, she's learning to tune in to her people and what they want. Plus she's starting to have fun with it. I mean, if you don't enjoy running your own business, you might as well go get a job working for the man!

My business buddy Kimra Luna is unique in the online marketing space. She has purple hair, tattoos, piercings and three of the cutest kids you've ever seen. Her direct, no bull, completely real approach is so much more than a breath of fresh air; she's like a bucket of ice over your head! Kimra attracts her own kind of rebels, misfits and aspiring entrepreneurs who are inspired by her rags to riches story, her no holds barred authenticity and her amazing knowledge.

Imagine if Kimra had tried to be like every other online marketer. Yawn. The success of her business is a direct result of putting herself front and center of her brand.

How to Create the Brand of You

- Is there something unique about you? It could be the story of how you ended up doing this, something you've overcome in your life, your background in another career. Try writing an About page for your business website and starting it with this story or fact.

- Do you have a particular vibe that makes you recognisable? It could be the way you look (hair dye and piercings or total vintage chic) or it could be a way of working. Try writing a description of your business in a couple of sentences, but imagine your business also has this vibe. How do you describe it?

No more bland. No more blending in. Let's embrace our uniqueness.

How do you do what you do? Is there something a bit different about you? If there is, why on earth would you hide it?

Lean into the Fear

When I first launched my coaching business, I struggled to find my niche. I had no idea how to differentiate myself from other coaches.

No matter how many clients I had, I couldn't shake the feeling that I was missing something and this lack of uniqueness was really holding me back. It bugged me. Every time I made a video, or wrote a blog, or posted on social media I got stuck questioning myself and everything I was going to say. I felt like I was in business limbo and unless I could crack the code, I'd never be able to step it up.

Rather than looking inside myself for answers, I looked everywhere else. All around me. The more I looked, the more my Facebook feed became chock-a-block with other business coaches humble bragging about their gorgeous, stylish, luxury, shiny beautiful lives.

It's not who I am at all! I even saw one woman doing some upside down yoga pose, in a bikini, by a beach, with a laptop. Hilarious. The idea that I could become a super glamorous business coach, living a life of luxury in cocktail dresses or in a bikini was completely laughable.

For a while I did wonder if I should try to fit the expectation of what a business coach is like; grow my hair, wear dresses and heels, that kind of thing.

But pretending to be something you're not is exhausting. People can see straight through your façade. For a start, I can't wear heels. I have the grace of an elephant that's been drinking. And I'm rarely seen out of my jeans and sneakers. I can't help it. That stuff is so not me. I knew I couldn't get away with being like that, it wouldn't wash and I had a feeling I'd probably fall flat on my face, literally.

It wasn't until someone very wise pointed out to me that the thing that makes me different was completely obvious; my voice.

They mentioned it. Just dropped it into the conversation.

I went quiet. What? I thought they were mad. I'd spent my whole life hiding from my voice, it was my biggest insecurity and I was hardly likely to bring it front and center now. I mean, why would I embrace the thing that I'd spent over 30 years trying to cover up?

There's a brilliant quote by mythology guru, Joseph Campbell which sums this up; "The cave you fear to enter holds the treasure you seek." Often the thing you're most scared of is THE thing; your big fat juicy thing!

I hid away for a while. No way was I going to open myself up to that level of ridicule. But the thought kept lurking there. In the back of the cave.

What if I did embrace my biggest insecurity? It scared the hell out of me. I got goosebumps just thinking about it. And that is usually a sign you're onto something.

And then one day, it hit me. My voice makes me feel little. And my people will get that. They'll know what it's like to feel little, to feel like you're holding yourself back and letting your fears and insecurities and doubts control you.

And that was it. I knew then that I had to do this. That embracing my little voice was the key to everything.

That night, as I was falling asleep, the name for my brand came to me. Little Voice Big Business. It occurred to me then and there whilst I was all warm and safe under my snuggly duvet that the ultimate challenge would be for me to launch a business podcast, and own my little voice completely.

Holy crap. A podcast, are you mad?!

But I did it. And it's been the making of me, and my business. My little voice in people's ears as they walk their dog, have a bath or go for a run. It's a special thing. And it's allowed me to really bond with my people.

What's the thing you're avoiding doing? Could that be the big thing that holds the key to your success? If you suspect you're avoiding doing it because you're afraid, ask yourself why. And take some time to explore it.

Your Story

When I pick up a magazine I always flick straight to the real life stories. Do you? I love reading about real people and their experiences. It's intriguing. Stories are an integral part of our culture. Religion is based on stories. We tell stories to our kids. It's why we read novels, watch TV and movies. Stories are everywhere. We tell stories to build trust, to calm our fears, explain the unknown and command respect.

The easiest way for you to uncover what makes you unique is to tell your story. I'm not talking about your entire life story, but the story of how you got here and came to be an expert at what you do.

If you consider that you've gone from point A to point B and now you're at point C, you have a story to tell. You don't need to be a Nobel Prize winner at your thing or the world's most renowned expert, you just need to be further along your journey than your clients. Remember that your clients are probably at point A and want to get to point B. You've been there and done it. So it's up to you to show them how. And demonstrate that you can get them there too.

★ ★ ★ CASE STUDY: ANUREET SRA ★ ★ ★
**Anureet Sra, a 5-to-9er balancing a full time career
with artistic and entrepreneurial activities
www.anureetsra.com**

I've been on quite a journey since I decided I wanted to run a business alongside my day job as an accountant. My entrepreneurial experience has reflected my multi-passionate personality. Everything I've done has taught me so much and led me on to the next step in my journey.

I started by training as a web designer and then started my business Couture Web. The business grew and became rather all encompassing! Looking back, I'm glad I learned these skills, but as my client work grew I realised that I wanted to move away from this kind of intensive, "done for you" work.

Then I created The 5-9er, to help people like me who are growing a business, whilst also working full-time. Rather than work with clients one to one, I've created something more scalable involving courses and online content. This format enables me to continue with my day job, help lots of people and still have time to pursue my true passion, art.

I've realised that although it's best to be focused on one thing, I can have a portfolio career. You may not end up where you thought you would, but if you don't even start on the journey, you won't get anywhere!

Bear in mind that your clients are where you used to be. So telling your story, your journey of how you got to be where you are now, will appeal to them, because they may want to do something similar.

If you've been through the mill and struggled at times, tell us about it. Don't try to gloss over it. Being vulnerable is human. It makes you relatable and honest which makes it easier for people to trust you.

So make like Netflix and keep your audience excited. Nobody wants to hear a chronological report of your entire life. Don't be the person that sends everyone to sleep. Put some drama in there! We want to hear how you charged at challenges, beat baddies, attacked adversity and fought failures. What did you do to turn things around? What action did you take? How did your life change as a result?

When I first started working with Linda Beach she told me a story from her childhood, of how her dad had taught her to strengthen her bravery muscles and how she'd walked away from a plane crash. Her whole life has been about fearless freedom. It's what makes her unique. Nobody else can tell the stories she can. While we were working together she was even inspired to get over her fear of flying—perfectly understanding after the plane crash—and she decided to leap out of a plane. Linda's journey is like nobody I've ever met. And her commitment to helping others live a life of fearless freedom is infectious.

The best part of a makeover is seeing the before and after. Your people are currently in the Before, dreaming of the After, and they are looking to you to help them achieve it. If you've managed to do it then they'll start to trust that you can help them to do it too.

★ ★ ★ CASE STUDY: KARAN DAY KAHL ★ ★ ★
Karan Day-Kahl, style therapist and sustainable fashion trader.

My business came from a need to heal myself. For some years, I had been working in the community sector with children in need and traumatized women, and I was burnt out.

On and off over the years I had enjoyed putting together outfits from the clothes in my wardrobe or in thrift stores, as a way of lifting myself out of sadness. I would experiment with putting this dress with that jacket or a blouse over a dress with a belt to bring it together. If I liked the look I would take a photo of the outfit. Then, on the days that I couldn't think of an outfit to wear, I would look at my look book and an outfit would be sorted.

It would always make me feel uplifted and ready to face my world, and I was also recycling, upcycling and keeping clothes out of landfill. A true win-win!

So KaransKloset began, at first at a local fashion market. Women of all different shapes and ages started asking me to stock different styles and sizes, and the business has developed into a recognised, sustainable fashion brand with a pop-up shop and regular customers.

Now, I'm taking my business online, and on to a whole new level, combining my love of style with my experience counselling women with low self-esteem and also those who have been abused.

Find Your Perfect People

You Deserve Magic

Your eyes meet and there it is; you can feel it. For a moment you can even hear the crackling of the electricity between you. If there were unicorns they would be dancing right now. That's what it feels like when you connect with one of your perfect people. It's thunderbolts a-go-go. Nothing can beat that fairy tale feeling.

A match made in business heaven is what we're aiming for, each and every time you connect with a client. You deserve to feel electricity.

It's the magic that happens when you find a client who is perfect for you. Someone who gets you, who is passionate about the things you believe in, who is looking for the exact help you can offer, and hopefully someone who you'd happily go for a drink with.

You deserve to feel this fuzzy feeling every time! When you run your own business you get to choose who you work with. That's one of the fabulous things about being an entrepreneur.

So why settle for less? Why put up with crappy behaviour?

We all know what it's like to date people who don't deserve us. I know that in the past I've tried to change people, endured untrustworthy behaviour and put up with less than stellar treatment. I've ignored my gut instincts on more than one occasion. And yet, rejecting someone can feel like an audacious and arrogant act.

We deserve to be around people who appreciate us and like us. You have full permission to say no to nightmare clients. We have a choice!

Tune into Your Tummy

I've learnt this the hard way. I've had that sense of dread and doom in my stomach on more than one occasion. And I've pressed the override button and ploughed on regardless. Deep down I've known that this person would end up being more trouble than they're worth. But, being a people-pleaser and not wanting to disappoint has always been my downfall, and as a result I've agreed to do things I never should have done. (I'm obviously talking about business here, right?)

I remember the first big client I won in my PR business. He popped up out of the blue and I was flattered that he'd found us when our business was so new. He had an interesting new product and he wanted me to help him market it. It was a big account, bigger than I'd secured before.

At our first meeting, I got a super creepy vibe off him. But I ignored it. Instead, focusing on the opportunity sitting in front of us. This was going to be massive for us!

We started to work together and things soon turn bad. What a shock!

After just two months, he turned extremely aggressive, refusing to pay unless we did more work, and more work and more work. Never mind that he had signed my extremely robust contract and that we were more than delivering. It turned out to be the job from hell, and it nearly destroyed the business.

In the end, wishing to prove a point, we sued him for breach of contract, in an effort to recoup the money he'd seemingly forgotten to pay. Preparing the legal papers took me weeks. It consumed my every waking thought. And it permeated my dreams too. I went full Law & Order. I really went to town. I was a woman possessed. Determined to prove we were right and he was in the wrong. As a result of the whole legal drama, I had less time to serve my other clients, let alone win more business. This one guy, this nightmare client from hell, could easily have toppled my business.

I remember the day we went to court. I was crapping myself. I'd built this guy up into such a baddie that I was convinced we were going to have some kind of brawl, ending in him stabbing me and leaving my lifeless body in a pool of blood. They'd call an ambulance, but it would be too late, and I'd just fade away, muttering incoherent stuff about his contract being water-tight.

And guess what. He didn't even show up. How he must have been laughing! The fact that we won the case, was neither here nor there. As the judge guy was telling us we'd won, an email plopped up onto his screen to notify us that he'd literally just liquidated the company that minute.

Do you think we got our money back? Ha! Of course we didn't! And could I let it go? No, of course I couldn't. I think I was traumatised for months afterwards. I kept imagining bumping into him in the street. And for months I continued to research him (stalk him more like) and I found out that he owed a lot of other people a ton of money and that in the scheme of things we had got off relatively lightly.

That little flippy-tummy feeling I'd had at the start was right all along. A lesson learned, the very hard way.

Working with the wrong clients can kill your business.

A Tale of Invoicing Hell

I'm certainly not alone in my experience of catastrophic clients... It happens all the time. Sometimes it can be the terms and conditions that get you in the end.

Michelle is an experienced and talented web designer. She loves her work. She can Java all night and all day. But things weren't always so rosy. Over a beer, Michelle told me the whole sorry saga of how her first business had collapsed in a heap of unpaid bills.

When she was first starting out, she had specialised in working for clients in the education sector and they had a rather rigid way of working, preferring to pay once the job was completed. Of course they did! They didn't like the idea of not having the completed website before they processed any invoices. The idea of paying online sent them into a cold sweat and to make matters worse they had a very complicated structure to their finance team. That's all well and good—for them.

But as a result of these conditions, it took Michelle over six months to get paid, every time. And often, the red tape was so scrambled, she would never get paid at all. To say Michelle experienced a cash-flow crisis would be rather an understatement. She ended up in all kinds of debt, and had to close the business, nearly losing her house.

I was outraged on Michelle's behalf. How could they do this to her? How dare they destroy a small business like that.

But in fact, the truth was much simpler than even Michelle would admit. The simple truth was, she let this happen. Because there's always a choice.

Choose Your Clients Carefully

Let's say it again; the joy of running your own business is that you can choose your clients.

Of course you want to please people, do a great job, change lives and make people happy. We all do. That's why we're here, serving our people.

But you don't have to accept any client who wants to work with you. You have to make a choice; a conscious decision whether this person is a good match for you.

Business is meant to be fun. (Well, I think it is!) And working with wrong'uns isn't fun, believe me. I've tried it, so you don't have to.

Just Say No

Here are some warning signs to look out for. If you get even an inkling that a potential client is exhibiting any of these signs, you have my full permission to say thanks, but no thanks, and promptly leg it in the opposite direction, arms flailing. Run for the hills!

Less than desirable clients have a habit of creeping up on us when we least expect it. Anyone can get clients, but you want splendid ones, not creepers. So we need to be vigilant and watch out for signs that a creeper may be approaching.

Creeper Client Checklist

- You get a bad feeling in your tummy when you think about them
- They slag off their last hire
- They're totally disorganised and all over the place
- They're not keen to commit
- They pressure you to start work before signing a contract
- They refuse to sign a contract altogether
- They haggle on price and question your fees
- They ask you to do 'sample' work before they make a decision, in effect getting you to do the work for free
- They don't know what they want
- They constantly change their mind

- They want a quick, easy, and above all, cheap solution
- They suggest you work for 'exposure', a referral, or a review, instead of money
- They have unrealistic expectations
- Their deadlines are ridiculously tight
- You're expected to be available 24/7
- They hound you with messages
- They don't turn up to meetings
- They're 'too busy' to do their part of the work
- They pay late, make excuses about paying or don't pay at all
- They completely disappear, ghosting your emails and calls

Do your existing clients behave like this? And if so, how do you think it's impacting your business? What are you going to do about it?

Local Isn't Always Best

Georgie makes gorgeous kids' clothing. She sells it locally at markets and fairs. The thing is, the people who live near Georgie don't really get it. They don't seem to understand her sense of style, and they certainly wouldn't "fork out" $30 on a baby romper suit.

These people are her friends, sure, but they're not her ideal clients. How do we know? Well, they don't buy her stuff. Not a sausage. And bit by bit, this constant questioning on price and rejection is eating away at Georgie's soul, not to mention her passion for baby fashion.

By focusing on the people she happens to live near, Georgie is allowing her business to be strangled.

But Georgie's people are out there. People who appreciate beautiful designs, who are willing to splash the cash on something truly gorgeous and unique. So she's starting to focus more on her online presence and less on local markets and fairs. This has given Georgie's sales a much-needed kick in the butt. She's found an audience who love her designs and are happy to pay for them.

Don't Let Local Kill Your Business

There's a whole big wide world out there for you. By focusing only on the people who happen to live round the corner from you, you're crushing your dreams.

We have the internet, man! And that gives us a huge amount of power and control over who we work with. Today, you get to choose who that is, no matter which tiny corner of the earth they happen to inhabit.

Finding Your Ideal Clients

We've looked at the kind of people you might want to avoid. But who do you actually want to work with?

I love my peeps. I love that I can spot them a mile off. I can be at an event and I can tell who's going to be my kind of person. As soon as we talk I just know.

I care about them. I want them to be successful. They're the kind of people I'd like to hang out with. They're fun. They get me. My stories resonate with them. We often have loads in common, from where we go on holiday to the films we love, our hobbies, even our sense of style. They also struggle with the things I struggle with, like feeling little or lacking confidence. They make running my business fun. I look forward to helping them and working with them. It's my purpose, my calling to help them and when we get results it makes me feel all happy and fuzzy.

There are plenty of professionals who seem to hate their clients. I often get that impression from the big boys in my industry. They seem to regard the people who pay for whatever program they're shifting as a bunch of muppets who don't know what they're doing. It's like they're a Disney cartoon with dollar signs in front of their eyeballs.

But working with clients you hate, or don't even respect, is not going to be enjoyable. And worse than that, you probably won't be making as much money as you would be working with the right people.

And I want you to have that magical connection with your clients because it makes working with them super fun.

Finding Clients: the Basics

Your ideal clients should:

- Need what you're offering
- Want to work with you
- Have money to spend—enough money!
- Behave professionally by paying on time, honouring contracts and taking action so that you can progress your work together.
- Be easy to find. If they're like hermits living in the hills, you're going to have a tricky time tracking them down.

Stick this little list of criteria on the wall, next to the list of things to avoid.

★ ★ ★ CASE STUDY: JUCI KISISTÓK ★ ★ ★
Juci Kisistók is a passive income strategist and tech VA
www.codeandglitter.com

Business was going OK. I was able to make a decent living, but I was feeling burnt out, confused and unmotivated.

I didn't really have a target audience and it showed! I was offering ALL the things to anyone who'd work with me. People were confused about what I really do and what I could do for them. But

I was scared that if I offered fewer services, or focused in on a particular niche, then I'd lose potential clients.

But I eventually realized that to get my motivation back I needed to find my people, and that meant I needed to niche down, reducing the number of services I offered.

Now, I work with rebels and changemakers who are tired of following the so-called rules of online business. I work closely with them to create websites that let their personalities shine, figuring out systems and passive income strategies that work for them.

When I made up my mind about what I really wanted to do and who I wanted to do it for, it all fell into place. It was almost magical!

The best thing about the online world is that you can meet awesome people from all around the world who will love your vibe and who you are, so don't be afraid to be as quirky as you want.

Ideal Client Checklist

- Do they need you?
- Do they want you?
- Do they have money?
- Are they easy to find?
- Do they behave well?
- Do you like working with them?

Once you're clear on this broad stuff, you can drill down to really specific criteria.

- Gender
- Age (roughly)
- Where they live (country, type of town etc)
- Interests & hobbies

- Type of work they do
- Where they shop
- What they're currently buying
- Books they're reading
- Where they're hanging out online
- Who they admire and follow e.g. gurus, coaches, authors
- What are they already buying to meet their needs?

I like to build a really clear picture of my people. Down to the kinds of magazines and books they read or the kinds of holidays they take. I wanna get under their skin. So I understand exactly what they're dreaming of!

You might be worried that if you get too specific you'll miss out on business. But this is a fallacy; by targeting a clear niche, you focus in on the right kind of clients, and you're more likely to attract more of them. Because everything you do is aimed at them, they will know immediately that you're for them. Because you get them. You talk directly to their interests and their desires, and it'll make them want to buy from you.

If you try to make yourself appeal to everyone, you risk not being particularly interesting to anyone.

★ ★ ★ CASE STUDY: SUSAN NELSON ★ ★ ★
Susan Nelson helps Christian women navigate the modern world.
www.womanofnoblecharacter.com.

Once I knew WHO my audience was and the value of what I had to offer, I became incredibly focused and cracked on with my strategy, content and launches. I hit the pavement hard! During my ideal client research calls, I realized that my program was needed and would be well-received. After all, I've experienced first hand the importance of choosing the right type of offering and learning the pain points of your target audience. I'm so excited about the future; growing my business, helping others, and making my dreams come true.

What Do They Really Want?

The most important thing we need to understand, and often the hardest to wrap our heads around, is what your people actually want.

At the risk of sounding like a parent here, there's a big difference between need and want. Jacob needs to brush his teeth but he doesn't want to. I need to eat healthily but I don't want to. I need to do the laundry, but I don't want to!

If your business is offering to meet a need, that's great. But unless your people actually want you to help them, then we're in trouble.

You might know that someone you've just met needs your decluttering service because their home is a mess, but they don't want it, because they'd rather spend their all their money on outfits for Monty, their micro pig.

The goal is to be sure that your product or service is something that people NEED, and which they would actually be willing to PAY for. Trying to flog something that nobody really wants is exhausting. If you wanted to spend your time wading through thick mud, you'd do one of those extremely arduous muddy obstacle course races.

Just because you feel called to teach cats Pilates, doesn't mean cats want to learn Pilates. Your business needs to be customer-centric if you want to make money, and that means that your client's dreams and desires matter more than yours. Sorry!

Once you know what someone dreams are, you can tailor your offering to meet those deepest desires. If someone dreams of living an organised life with less stress, then pitch it in the right way and they will *want* that decluttering service.

So how can you find this stuff out? Go talk to your people!

Key Questions

- What problem do they want to solve in their lives / work?
- How is this affecting their life?
- How important is it that they do something to fix it?
- What are their dream and desires? What do they really, really want?
- What does an ideal situation look like to them? What's the dream scenario?
- What's stopping them from achieving this?
- What would it mean to them if they could achieve this goal?

Be Prepared to Pivot

If you've been bashing away at your business for a while and no matter what you do or try, it's just not working, it could be that you're looking in the wrong place for your perfect people.

It may be time to pivot. Pivoting means changing the focus or direction of your business to follow an opening in the market, possibly one you didn't realise existed until you started out.

Imagine you've been promoting your social media services to weasel breeders for, like, forever, and you're getting nowhere. You realise that in reality weasel breeders are few and far between, and the breeders there are aren't actually interested in outsourcing their social media because they prefer to spend their budget on weasel food.

But what if you switched focus away from weasels?

Maybe you'll have more success offering social media management services to furry-fashionista-focussed businesses. You're still keeping the core of your business—social media management—but you're pivoting to target a new customer demographic.

When I first met Jess she was helping kindergarten managers to grow their businesses. She's fantastic at her work, but after plugging away at it for a few months it became apparent that this niche was not going to be an easy one. People didn't seem to want help, and their budgets were barely visible to the naked human eye. Happily, Jess was able to pivot and find a much more promising bunch of people to work with. She focused on her organizational skills but found a new customer base for them; she now runs a successful virtual assistance business with a consistent flow of clients. People come to her because of her amazing reputation and they pay her properly for her work. Marvellous.

Just Imagine

Imagine how fun work will be when you're working with your perfect people. People you understand. You get what they want. And you're best placed to give it to them. The ease and flow and joy. Not to mention the mutual respect and the fact that you'll get paid. On time. In full. They appreciate you and you appreciate them. And who knows, if they're super happy they may even recommend you to their friends.

★ ★ ★ CASE STUDY: CAROLINE M WOOD ★ ★ ★
Caroline M Wood is a Facebook ad strategist and trainer
www.carolinemwood.com

My business helping foodie businesses with their finances wasn't going anywhere. Money was going out and none was coming in. I was spending hours on it, but it had just stalled; I was starting to resent it and was on the point of giving up on it completely.

I realised that I was working in a niche where people don't spend much money. Something had to change. And that something was my entire business!

I looked at the skills I had that people would pay for, and I realised that my Facebook ads management and training skills were in huge demand. And I ended up specialising even further; I decided that the type of clients I want to work with are women who are at the early stages of their business. Getting to this point has made it so much easier to come up with packages and services that work for them and meet their needs.

After feeling like I had been hitting my head against a brick wall trying to find clients with my first business, now I was winning clients. It felt amazing. I felt like I had a business that would actually work.

It's so important to get clear on who you serve and how. And you have to talk to people. I tried to do everything through online research, but nothing beats actually talking to real people to identify something that adds value to them.

Since making the switch I have slowly grown my business to the point where I quit my 9-5 to focus on it full time. My Aha! moment came when I finally processed the fact that I wasn't just on leave, that I didn't have to go back to the office ever again. It brought such a sense of contentment and relief.

Love Me Long-Time

People are more important than numbers. This may sound counter intuitive, particularly because this is a business book and you're probably reading it because you want to make more money, but the moment we forget we're here to serve our clients, that's when our business falls apart. Treating people like just another notch on your bedpost, is guaranteed to send them running off to a more appreciative business.

If you get dollar signs in front of your eyeballs whenever you think about your people, it may be time to have a harsh word with yourself. Let's reign in those mercenary tendencies and focus instead on creating long-term loving relationships with your peeps. Because, if you focus on your people and put them at the center of everything you do, the money will follow.

The moment you become obsessed by the size of your list, the number of clients you have, or the amount of money you're making, that's the moment you lose focus on what really counts. It's not just about numbers, and the number of people through the door, it's about the results they get from you, and whether they choose to stick around and keep coming back for more.

Make Me Feel Special

I recently signed up for a really rather expensive group program for my business. Partly I wanted to see what the fuss was all about, but I was also just in the mood for a fresh perspective and some accountability.

After a few weeks, I met the person running the program in person, at an event we were both speaking at. I was all like, hey there! I'm on your program! It's so good to meet you!

I was so excited to connect with this person and felt really honoured to be on the same panel as her. I wanted to gush and tell her all about my business and let her know how happy I was to meet her.

Except she didn't seem to care.

It was such a let down. I couldn't shake the feeling that this person couldn't give a damn about me.

There was a mismatch between our expectations. I'd spent a chunk of money on this program, and it was important to me. But for her, I was just one of hundreds of people who'd paid her, and it didn't matter to her who else I was.

In the end I cancelled and asked for a refund. I didn't feel like I could carry on with someone who seemed so uninvested in me, especially after I'd given them a few thousand dollars of my hard-earned. Screw that.

If you want your clients to stick around, make them feel special. Show interest, ask questions, reply to their emails. Even if you're having a bad day, make an effort! A smile and a nice comment costs nothing and it goes a long way to making someone feel loved and appreciated.

And it's not about doing the bare minimum and smiling at people through gritted teeth as you count up your money. It's about making your people into heroes. Show them how much you appreciate them, and rate them, and love them. Celebrate their achievements and their wins. Shout it from the rooftops, or in your emails, videos or social media.

Your super fans can be a marketing team for your business on a massive scale. Give them stories to share. The more successful they are, the more successful you will be.

The Dating Game

Client relationships are not so different to dating. You spot each other on Tinder, you feel the magic, those unicorns start singing.

You spend lazy days looking into each other's eyes. You feel like you can see into their soul, tune into their deepest desires. You know what they want from life. You're committed to supporting them in achieving their ambitions. You know what worries them. What keeps them up at night.

Your relationship is based on mutual respect. Both your lives are better because you're together. Over time, the trust and connection builds and builds until finally you're ready to do the do, make a commitment and settle down.

But like a marriage, a business relationship takes time and effort to build. It's not about going in hard, trying to get what you can. You show them you care, you listen, you're helpful. If you want the long-term, you can't rush things. You have to woo them.

Dating is Expensive

The trouble is, going on lots and lots of first dates costs a bomb. New outfits, dinner, drinks, taxis—it all adds up! And the same goes for business. Have you ever considered how much time, effort and money goes into acquiring a new customer? Your cost of acquisition is probably a lot higher than you realise.

Think about it; you've got to factor in, for example, time spent travelling to a networking event, petrol, the time you spend in the meeting, and any marketing materials you hand out, plus membership fees if you have to pay to be there. Whether you use this more traditional method, or you're paying for online ads and spending hours tweeting away on social media, getting a client involves cost. And no matter how much you're spending, or what you're spending it on, it costs a hell of a lot more to acquire a new customer than it does to retain an existing one. By continually having to find more and more new clients, you're wasting time, money and energy.

Your Business is Not a Brothel

Your milkshake may bring all the boys to the yard, but will they come back for another one? You don't want to run your business like a drop in center where people just pop in for a quickie whenever they feel like it. That's not gonna make your mamma proud.

Constantly chasing after new clients and then letting them wander off makes no sense at all. It's like you're filling a bucket, but it has a big hole in the bottom of it. Drip, drip, drip. You're never going to grow your business if you're running hard on the spot.

Rather than just focusing on how to seal the deal; we're going to approach this with a more loving, in-it-for-the-long-haul approach. I get that customer experience isn't as glamorous and sexy as sales, but it's what successful businesses are built on. And that's why we're here, right?

Long-Term, Loving Relationships

So what's the alternative? Instead of allowing money to leak through your fingers, we're going to leverage each client relationship and turn you from the master of the one-night-stand to someone who has a whole family of long-term loving clients.

Here are some more changes you can implement in your business, that will help you to make this long-term loving customer experience a reality in your business.

Setting Boundaries

If you're making it easy for people to hook up with you with no strings attached, then it's time we built some boundaries for your business. Serious, long-term relationships require commitment and are founded on mutual respect.

So, if you're giving it all away on the first date, for free, of course you're not getting second helpings. Does this sound familiar? If so, it sounds like you may have had a boundary bypass. These are the telltale signs:

- You're often asked if people can 'pick your brains' on your area of expertise
- When you try to sell, you're so keen that you throw in stuff for free
- People only ever seem to want to book you for a one-off session
- Clients try to haggle you down on price
- Projects leak over the edges until they're completely out of control
- You're often asked to help with things you don't specialise in

I'm not judging you. I've been there!

I was once invited to my local bar for a business meet-up. When I got there, there was no one else there apart from the organizer, who was a nutritionist. Where were the others? Oh they couldn't make it, she said. Caught unawares, I didn't see what was coming and sat down, but I had inadvertently stumbled into brain-sucking trap. I may as well have had my grey matter attached to the beer tap, as she pumped me dry. Three hours later I stumbled home, wrung out. I'd given away thousands of dollars of advice, in exchange for a beer and a packet of peanuts. I had let that happen to me. It was my fault. I vowed never to let that happen to me again.

To avoid this kind of biz-mess, we're going to put some boundaries in place.

If you want to run a business that makes money, so you can keep doing what you do, the time has come to get a little bit strict. A few years ago I would have shied away from fortifying my business fences. I would have thought it seemed a bit mean.

But having experienced some pretty major business disasters along the way, I've realised that this stuff is not only going to protect you and your business, it's also going to improve your customer experience. If there are no boundaries laid out, it's very easy for things to get out of hand.

When I was first starting out with my coaching business, I thought I could turn my hand to anything. And it ended up getting me in a right mess.

I started coaching a local woman on how to scale her business. It became clear from the beginning that her website was holding her business back. It was chaotic and was creating work rather than helping her drive sales. At the end of our sessions together she turned to me and thanked me for my work, but she asked what she could do about the website. Oh, and she didn't have the budget to hire a web designer.

She pleaded with me to help her. I wanted her to like me. I knew how to do a bit of web design. I crumbled. And I offered to help. What a fool.

It turned into the project that would never end. Instead of simply changing the theme and adding a few plugins to her site, as I'd imagined, it snowballed. I was in way over my head and it nearly killed me. In fact, I nearly killed her.

I learned my lesson the hard way, that's for sure. Only offer your services on things that you're expert in. Don't get sidetracked or talked into doing things that you don't normally do, even if someone begs you to help them.

Here are some suggestions for things you can implement right now to build better boundaries in your business.

1. Discovery calls
If someone needs your help, book them in for a discovery call with you, to see if you're a good fit for working together. When they book in, they'll need to answer a series of qualifying questions to check they're a good fit. This will help you avoid time-wasters.

If they want to meet up for a chat and a coffee, you will only give them 30 minutes of your time and it's up to you to run the conversation like a discovery call.

We'll go into this in more detail later in the book, but essentially it's up to you to listen to them and suggest HOW you WOULD help them if you were to work together. You're NOT actually going to do the work for them then and there. Not under any circumstances! This is a sales conversation and should ultimately end in you closing the deal.

2. Clear Scope
When someone agrees to work with you, avoid unrealistic expectations (which lead to complaints) by being super clear about what they can expect and when. It's all about managing expectations. Without a clear scope it's so easy to get sucked into a spiral of client carnage! I've seen this play out and it's not pretty, believe me.

Avoid doing more and more work for free as you respond to a never-ending list of "can you just's." Make it crystal clear how many amends, reviews, emails, updates and so on they can expect.

Lay out what will happen once those options have been exhausted. Can they hire you for additional hours at a set rate, or do they need to upgrade to a more premium package?

How will you both know when the project is finished? Don't get lured into a never-ending nightmare that takes over your life!

3. Communication Channels

Make it clear how you like to be contacted, when you'll be available to them and how long typically it might take you to respond. If you don't want clients sending you messages on Facebook, tell them.

Set clear office hours. Just because you're checking your phone on a Sunday night doesn't mean you're going to respond to clients instead of watching The Good Wife. Your clients need to know that you have a life, that you're not there at their beck and call 24/7.

4. Contract

Every client relationship needs a legally binding contract that you and your client signs before work commences.

Your contract should detail the scope of your work as well as payment terms, disclaimers and circumstances under which the contract may be terminated. Don't just make the contract up, make sure it would stand up in court if the situation arose.

It may cost you money to get a solid contract written up but it will save you a lot of money and heartache in the long run. Even if you trust your client, or you happen to be friends, you still need to do this!

★ ★ ★ **CASE STUDY: SADAF SOLANGI** ★ ★ ★
Sadaf Solangi, massage therapist
www.earthrosemassage.com

Although I was getting clients through word-of-mouth recommen-dations, the business wasn't working as well as it could. Clients would sometimes not turn up, or ask to book a session on my day off. I had no cancellation policy and my prices were too low. I was not making a profit.

Over the past few months I've got more confident in my own abilities and introduced boundaries to help me run a more profitable business. Now I have raised my prices, I have a cancellation policy, I take a deposit and I don't allow people to haggle on price. I don't work on my days off and I don't work with people who bring my energy down.

And now I realise that my ideal clients are happy with all those boundaries. In fact, it makes them feel more secure too.

I don't feel overwhelmed any more. I feel like a real entrepreneur and someone who is in control of their destiny. I'm excited to take my business to the next level!

★ ★ ★

Creating Packages

If you're allowing people to look elsewhere as soon as they've swiped right on your business, if clients are demanding instant results on the spot without appreciating the work involved, then you need some big package action.

We're going to move away from one-time interactions and package up your business into offerings that encourage clients to stick around for longer and get better, deeper, more impactful results.

Most importantly, offering packages instead of ad hoc interactions will enhance the results you get for your clients. But an added bonus is that it will also leverage your client relationships and ramp up your revenue.

It's impossible for me to do great work in a 30-minute session. I can do something, sure … but real results take time. And I for one am not keen to work with people who are just after a quick fix.

There are different ways of creating packages—for example, monthly retainers, a 12-week package, a membership. The format you choose depends on the work you're doing and what will suit your people best.

The key to creating a successful big package is to focus on the results they are likely to achieve; the outcome. This needs to be something life changing, something they dream about and are willing to invest their hard-earned cash in.

For example, if I had a skin care business helping clients who struggle with eczema, I would introduce a VIP monthly retainer. I'd make it clear that after their initial session, I only work with people who are committed to taking care of their skin long term. I'd explain that getting rid of eczema and having beautiful skin requires a level of care and commitment that I can only achieve if I work with my clients on a regular basis.

If I were a fitness instructor, I wouldn't allow clients to just turn up to my classes when they felt like it. Instead I would create a 12-week program designed to improve core strength and create the beginnings of a six-pack. I'd expect my clients to sign up for the full 12-week program. I might ask them to pay me in two instalments, once before the first session, and once half-way through the program.

In both examples, I'm engineering a long-term relationship that gives my business stability and a recurring customer base, but that also adds value for the client and achieves the results they really want.

If someone wants to work with you, and they're committed to getting results, they need to invest their time and money in achieving that goal. No more attracting people who are only willing to spend a few quid and an hour of their time.

★ ★ ★ CASE STUDY: CLAUDINE WEEKS ★ ★ ★
Claudine Weeks is a copywriter and content creator
www.igwdigital.com

When I started out I was charging by the hour. It was almost a finger in the air approach, which I quickly realised doesn't work for every client. So I developed a series of packages, taking a very flexible approach and tailoring them to each client according to their needs.

I now have one-off start-up packages for new businesses. I have monthly support packages for big corporates and ongoing packages for web designers who want to work with me in a partnership.

As a result of changing my charging structure like this I have secured more clients, which is amazing. My first month in business brought in $79—last month I hit $10k!

Logical Next Step

How long do your clients tend to stick around for? Do you even know? When someone finishes working with you, what happens next?

If you spend ages wooing people and then just let them wander off once they've finished your course or program or package, you're chucking money out the window. You've spent all that time building trust, getting results for them and now you're just going to let them walk away?!

The answer is to create a logical flow between products. When someone comes to the end of a program or package, it makes sense to offer them something else, to continue that relationship. This helps you maintain long-lasting relationships and as a result, make more money.

BIG
PROFIT

Go Figure

Do sums and spreadsheets give you the heebie jeebies? If you get a feeling of fear and dread when it comes to numbers, you're not alone. It turns out math anxiety is actually a thing! The trouble is, if you avoid getting to grips with your cashflow, your business will fail to flourish and may even die on it's ass. It's time to grow a pair and make friends with your figures. How can you make more money in your business, if you have no idea what's going on? You can't. That's how.

I have something to confess. Promise you won't tell anyone? I'm severely allergic to accounts. There I said it!

It all stems from my first graduate job; where I became known as the world's worst trainee accountant. Of all the career choices in all the world, this seems to have been the most ill-suited choice of all. In fact, it's an absolute wonder that they gave me a job at all. But, that's a story for another day.

Actually, let's not leave it there, I don't want you to think that I got up to something untoward.

A few miserable hours at a 21st birthday party, surrounded by very smug school friends, was all it took for me to abandon my vague sense of self and come to the conclusion that a career in accountancy was my calling in life. I'm embarrassed to say that it only took three beers for me to make this decision, on the basis that I wanted to wear a suit to work, earn enough money to buy nice things, get my own apartment and pretend to be all grown up and sensible. Unfortunately, the reality of my first foray into "adulting" was a disaster.

Turns out, I'm not great with detail. Or rules. Who knew?! And spending week after week holed up in an airless, windowless office with only 4,000 dusty lever arch files for company is not my cup of tea, in the slightest.

Much to my surprise, given my job title included the word "audit," I spent eight hours a day trawling through file after file, er... auditing stuff. (Note to self; I really ought to have got down with the lingo before I applied for the job.) I just couldn't take it. I took every available opportunity to rebel. I went kerazzee, using multi-colored pens and symbols in my checking system. On a particularly wild day I would even use animals and faces. Halcyon days, they were not. Throw accountancy exams into the mix and you have a very unhappy Nadia indeed.

Now, all these years later, the thought of doing my accounts brings me out in hives. Well not quite, but you get the picture. It would be oh so easy for me to use my loathing of accounts as an excuse. But, I'm an entrepreneur, so I can't. I have to give myself a clout with a large calculator, and tell myself to get a grip.

And so do you.

It's amazing how often I meet entrepreneurs who are in complete denial about their numbers. Ignorance is not bliss. Far from it! Not knowing doesn't mean it's not happening, dude. In fact, living in fear of your figures is going to cause real problems for your business.

You may be tempted to skip this chapter, but please, DON'T! It might not be the most fun you've ever had, you'll be so glad you did it, I promise.

★ ★ ★ CASE STUDY: REBECCA MILLER ★ ★ ★
Rebecca Miller is a publicity coach for entrepreneurs
www.writeandreach.com

I'm a words person - finances and money has always freaked me out, so much so that it became a dirty word. But my business was ticking along, I had an email list which was bringing me clients, slowly but surely, so I thought it was OK. I'd created some course materials for a package a few years ago but I had failed to really do the sums and calculate how many people to expect to join when I only had a small list. I was spending too much time meeting clients for 'coffee and a chat'—unbilled! Lovely as this was, it certainly wasn't paying the bills. I wasn't bringing enough clients, or enough money to maintain my lifestyle. Some months were great but others were mediocre; I was trapped in a boom-bust cycle.

I realised that I needed to really sort out my finances if I was going to run a successful business. I repackaged my course materials into an academy format and started offering monthly support packages. I started keeping better records, so that I don't have that last minute panic when then tax return is due, and actually looking at my forward plan, thinking about how much money I need to bring in each month, and what I can do to make that happen.

It's really helped me to get focused on what packages work for me, and on growing my membership.

In It for the Money

You have a passion. A message you want to share with the world. Lives you're going to change. Expertise you feel compelled to share. And that's awesome. But this is a business. It's not a project. Or a hobby.

In order to continue doing what you love and helping your people, you need to make money.

It's not about being greedy, or money grabbing, it's about creating impact and a sustainable business. The more money you make the more people you can help.

You deserve to be paid. Just because you're doing something you love doesn't mean you deserve to be paid any less. Work can be fun. It's not about punishing yourself.

If you get paid properly for your work, you'll have more energy and enthusiasm to keep doing it. Besides, if you're making good money, you'll be paying tax and supporting society as a whole and you'll be able to give money to charity.

Your Big Ones

When someone joins my group program, The Profit Pack, one of the first things we do together is go through their numbers. I call that module Band Aid, because it's painful to rip it off, but once you've done it, things can only get better. So let's do it now; who knows, perhaps it won't be as bad as you think.

Even those of us with the biggest number aversion can cope with just four numbers, right? Because there are really only four numbers that you absolutely have to keep on top of in your business.

1. Monthly Income. How much money do you bring in each month?
2. Monthly Costs. How much money do you spend each month?

3. Cash. How much cash do you have in the bank?
4. Profit. How much money are you able to keep each month—before tax?

These four pieces of information will give you a clear sense of what's going on in your business. You'd never go for a run with your eyes closed would you? Well, without these four numbers you're running your business blind and could easily run straight into a lamppost. Smack.

Once you know what these numbers are, you can use them to check on the health of your business. You can use them to make sure that:

1. Your monthly income goes up each month.
2. Your costs are a lot less than your income.
3. You have enough cash in the bank to pay your bills—including your tax.
4. Your profit is large enough to make this whole business worth doing!

You Need a Big Tool

If you don't already have one, you're gonna need a sensible money management system—not just scraps of paper strewn all over the house and stuffed down the back of the sofa.

You can either keep a spreadsheet and check your bank balance a few times a week, or you could use a swanky money management software option. You can pick one with a smartphone app that will give you an overview of your business at a glance wherever you are, at any given moment. In my experience, this kind of software can actually make doing your finances fun. Who'd have thought it? I love seeing the little graph go upwards each month, and getting notifications that I've been paid. Kerching!

Take a look at software systems such as Freshbooks, Xero or Quickbooks, which do all kinds of whizzy things to save you time, hassle and meltdowns. For example;

- Reconcile bank data and Paypal stuff automatically—no more having to type stuff in yourself.
- Send an invoice with a click of a button. Never again forget to get paid!
- Automated payment reminders ensure you get paid on time.
- Track and organize expenses in the Cloud. No more shoeboxes for you.
- Cool reports that show you where your business stands in an instant.
- A smartphone app you can access wherever you are, so you can track your business on the bus or on the beach.
- No more losing stuff! Your data will be stored in the cloud, and backed up safely.

★ ★ ★ CASE STUDY: CORRINA JELLEYMAN ★ ★ ★
Corrina Jelleyman is a remedial and therapeutic bodyworker, mentor and wellbeing coach.
www.backtotouch.co.uk

I had gotten into a rut in my business. Client appointments were irregular and I wasn't really doing any marketing to get myself out there. I was making a profit, but nowhere near what I was capable of doing.

When I'm in my treatment room, I LOVE what I do. I feel like this is what I'm meant to be doing to make a difference in the world.

I wanted to grow my business, but I didn't want to lose that personal connection. The only way forward I could see was to be working more hours. And there weren't more hours available in the day! At least, not if I wanted to see my children. All I could see in the future was a stressed mum, just about surviving financially, but getting nowhere fast.

I realized that I had to face my current financial situation. It was like a benchmark; if I knew where I was, I would be able to tell when I moved forward.

I had to make a mental shift and recognise that this was not a hobby. I needed to make the change from "mummy who also did some massage" to "business owner and working mum."

Firstly, I let go of the activities in my business that were draining my time and energy but not making me money. I also worked on finding money leaks, a bunch of things I was paying for but not using, so I cut them out, freeing up money for me to use to grow my business.

Since then I've stopped playing small. I'm completely focussed on the things that have the best return on investment. Now, I think of myself as the CEO of my business. I have pushed past my fears with action.

Get Paid

Cash flow is the amount of cold hard cash your business has coming in and going out. There's an old saying 'turnover is vanity, profit sanity and cash reality'—and how true it is. It's one thing to be on track to make lots of money, but unless it lands in the bank on time and when you need it then you're in the danger zone.

Cash flow problems are the single biggest business killer. Bury your head in the sand at your peril! Even if your business is making money, if you're not on top of cash flow you might find yourself in a tricky situation when a bill comes in unexpectedly and you don't have the ready money you need to pay.

Those pesky 30-day payment terms written in small print at the bottom of invoices can prove lethal. Big businesses often try to hold on to cash for as long as possible, and will therefore pay you later than you'd like. This means that you're left waiting for payment, with bills of your own to pay. Without careful cash flow management and an eagle eye on your bank balance, your whole business could go belly up quicker than you can say "cash flow crisis".

Here are my cash flow tips to help you stay alert and be aware of the amount of cash in your business at all times:

- Check your bank balance and sales forecasts at least weekly so you can see if anything is about to go wrong.
- Put a warning system in place so that, if you get dangerously close to running out of money, your bank lets you know.
- Keep a cash buffer for a rainy day, or see if your bank will give you a free overdraft facility.
- Make sure you write your payment terms clearly at the bottom of your invoices.
- Consider invoicing a percentage of any fees up front and the rest on completion.
- Make it easy for people to pay you—take payment over the Internet or over the phone where appropriate.
- Ask your clients to pay for materials or send an up-front payment to enable you to pay for stuff.
- Keep hold of cash in your business for as long as possible—whilst simultaneously trying to get people to cough up as quickly as possible. I like to think of it as a kind of grip and grab move. As soon as you make any money, bank it.

- Only pay your own bills when they are due—don't pay in 15 days, if the terms are 30 days.
- Charge interest on late payments.
- After a couple of days, if money hasn't been paid, call the client to chase. Don't be shy.
- Credit-check your customers to make sure they will pay you and they'll pay on time.
- Refuse to work with slow paying clients or insist they pay up front.
- Offer discounts for clients who pay early to encourage good payment behavior.
- If someone continues to pay late, stop working with them. A late payer can turn into a non-payer.

Profit is King

Entrepreneurs sometimes seem to have a screwy relationship with spending. Like we've forgotten that profit is what really counts.

I'm so over hearing about people who are generating seven figures or more. As if that's the benchmark of success! Have you ever stopped to wonder how much they spent to get there?

Spending a million to make a million is not that impressive, is it? The general idea is to make more money than you spend. It's all about PROFIT!

I'm assuming that you'd quite like to keep some money at the end of each month to spend on fun things, so it's time to take a look at your spending.

All the Gear, no Idea

You might have a super spiffy website featuring gorgeous lifestyle photography and an amazing logo, but if you're not actually making any money what's the point? You'd be surprised how often I see this happening. It's like running a business has got tangled up with a shopping spree. Put the credit card away, people. Don't be the person with all the shiny new equipment who looks awesome, but never turns a profit.

Remember that good enough is good enough. You can always upgrade your basic website for something shinier and fancier later on when you're making more money. Arguably you could go out there and get clients without even having a website, a logo, or any photography. It's important, but not essential. So, if you can't afford it for now, keep hold of your cash.

Spend a Penny

But what if you're more of a Scrooge than a shopaholic? Is your non-existent budget buggering up your business?

Running a business costs money. There's no getting away from it. But while some of us are spending too much, others attempt to run a business without spending a penny. This is one of my personal bugbears. Grrrr.

Wasting weeks fiddling with a web page that someone could fix in a day, because you can't pay for help, strikes me as crazy. If your toilet broke you'd get someone in, you wouldn't spend three weeks with your head down the loo trying to botch something together would you? Please tell me you wouldn't!

If you're the kind of person who doesn't like spending money, consider how it's holding you and your business back. If you're spending all your time doing stuff someone else could do more quickly (and probably better) if you paid them to, your competitors are going to out-run you. If you know that paid Facebook ads are the easiest and most effective way to grow your customer base, then do it! Don't spend years trying to build things organically for the sake of saving a few hundred dollars.

I'm not advocating getting into debt. No way. But it might be a good idea to get some money coming in from a part-time job or some additional freelancing on the side to help you get things moving. Wasting months and even years going at a snail's pace because you can't afford to pay for a web designer, or the stand at that key trade show, or that piece of equipment you really need, is madness. It's a false economy. It's one thing not to waste money, but quite another to hold yourself back.

Scale Up

The kid's party was a sugar-fuelled frenzy, with screaming to rival a Justin Bieber concert. Not my idea of a fun time. But you've gotta do what you've gotta do!

To escape the mayhem, I got talking to Jo, one of the other moms, and it turned out she was starting a business, as a beauty therapist.

Things were going really well, although it was early days. Jo was feeling pretty positive about the future. But as she talked and told me all about her plans, I got that uneasy feeling in my tummy.

I'd heard all this before and I could see exactly where Jo and her business was heading; a life of crazy hours and tiny profits.

Charging $40 an hour. One off sessions, as and when people book in. Paying $20 to hire a room.

As I munched away on birthday cake, I did the numbers. (In my head, obviously. I'm not a complete party pooper!)

Working part-time around the kids and leaving time for admin, updating her notes, invoicing and all that stuff, the maximum number of clients she could realistically see in a day was four. (4 x $40 = $160 per day)

If Jo works four days a week she would make $640 a week, or roughly $2560 a month—and that's if she never goes on holiday, her kids never get sick and she never needs to take time away from her business. Considering that most of her clients only book in once a month, Jo would need a hell of a lot of clients to make enough to live on.

And more to the point, $2560 is a long way from replacing the $5k per month she used to earn in her job.

You can see why I had that sinking feeling when she was telling me about her big plans. This is a pattern I see all the time; one that leads to working crazy hours for tiny profits.

There has to be an alternative. A way for us to work less and earn more, so we can hit those $5k, $10k or even $20k months without burning out or falling out of love with our business.

There are things you can do to stop this happening to you. Things like:

- Putting up your prices. (And having the confidence to do so)
- Creating packages of services.
- Leveraging your time through group programs or memberships.
- Creating products that you sell over and over again.
- Automating your systems to save you time.

And that's just for starters!
All this is possible.

I know, because I used to be in the $100 for a one-off session trap. I also used to regularly let sessions overrun, so my hourly rate was instantly cut in half.

What a wally.

I made some big changes in the way I do business, using all action points above. Now, I get paid when I go to the spa. I get paid when I'm out with my friends. And it's fab.

I want this for you too.

If you're sick of working crazy hours for tiny profits, you need to make changes so that you hit those $5k months, without working any harder.

It's time to stop selling time for money. Time to stop being limited by the length of your day and the number of squares in your diary.

Time to move from running your business, like you're a freelancer, and step it up to create a global brand.

I promise it's not as scary as it sounds. We do it by leveraging your time and expertise, by creating products and programs that allow you to work with lots of people at one time and elevate a one-to-one service to a VIP offering.

No matter what you do or how you do it, there are things we can do to make your business more profitable, and work harder for you—so you don't have to.

It's What You Know

It used to be that businesses were either product based or service based. You sold a product, a tangible item, or you sold a service, something you did.

But times have changed and the lines between product and service have become blurred. If you run what would traditionally be called a service business, the key to making more money and scaling up is productification. OK, I made that word up, but seriously, what we're aiming for is to create a mixture of products and services.

Services take time—your time. And there's only so much of it to go round. Unless you want to start taking on staff, then a pure service business puts a limit on how much money you can make.

But a product can be sold over and over again, and it's not tied to how much time you have. So we need to turn your services into products.

If you're an expert at something, you're helping your people to solve a problem. You're selling knowledge, and that knowledge is your intellectual property, unique to you. And knowledge can be packaged up into products. Doing this enables you to share your knowledge with loads more people, without necessarily being there in person. That's scaling up.

While you're delivering the service side of your business, people can be consuming your products and learning stuff from you. And paying you. You create content and it works hard for you over and over again, instead of you selling your time for money.

By packaging up what you know into products you're able to help more people. Partly because tens, hundreds, hell, thousands of people can be learning from you at once, but also because you've become more accessible. Not everyone can afford to work with you one-to-one, but lots more people will be able to pay you a monthly membership fee or a one off payment of a couple of hundred dollars. They'll still get results.

The chances are you have a way of teaching people. A method. But you might not have identified it as such. Once you have identified it and turned it into a product, you've created a process that someone else can follow and use to make a change in their lives. You could even teach other people how to use it to train even more people. That's how to scale.

Once you've come up with this 'how to' framework, everything revolves around it. It makes life a lot easier, partly because you're not wasting time rethinking and reinventing the wheel each time you make anything, but also because people start to understand what you're all about.

You can use your how-to skeleton to create courses, books, podcasts, talks, webinars, programs… all the things.

But how do you do it?

★ ★ ★ CASE STUDY: LOUISE COWLEY ★ ★ ★
**Louise Cowley is the founder of online graphic
design platform for female entrepreneurs.**
designsta.com

I was working as a freelance graphic designer, trying to build up my client base. One of my main clients was a London agency—they had very cool, world-renowned clients and I was really thrown in at the deep end with crazy deadlines, long hours and very demanding briefs. At first I was buzzing to be forging a career in design, each brief was exciting and the ideas were flowing but it wasn't long before I started to feel frazzled, the 1am phone calls from clients wanting "slight tweaks" or "just a quick amendment—it'll only take you two seconds" were grinding me down.

I was sick to death of trading time for money. I was sick to death of not making the money that I felt like I deserved for all the hours I was putting in.

At the same time I was noticing a trend in the online circles I was mixing in. More and more female entrepreneurs were doing their own design work, DIY style. They didn't have any design training, but sites like Canva or PicMonkey were making it possible for them to get professional-looking results. I realised that there was the makings of a super-scalable design service business here.

My idea, Designsta was launched in 2015; an online graphic design platform and members' club for female entrepreneurs. Members can log into the site and design anything they need for their business, from social media images to printables or workbooks and much more.

The site offers easy-edit templates that entrepreneurs can change to suit their branding. There are training videos and bundles and a strong support element via the Designsta Classroom Facebook group where I give personal feedback during 'Studio Hours'.

I've had to make decisions about prioritising my time. It's a super-scalable business model but I didn't want to jeopardise being able to give attention to all of my members, so I have set days and times where people can ask me questions and I can set aside the time to go through them all and help them out. And I've scaled back some packages and offers that required too much regular input from me, and delegated some tasks like Facebook advertising to an expert instead of doing it myself. Tweaking and testing is definitely key!

I earn money while I sleep now. It's amazing to get those payment notifications coming through on my phone at all hours of the day and night wherever I am in the world. The greatest thing for me is the huge amount of satisfaction I feel at getting to design the stuff I love, and having members all over the world using those designs in their business.

A Clear Goal

The first step is to work out the goal you're helping your customers to achieve. Do they want to decorate dogs? Shear sheep? Learn how to box like Anthony Joshua? The goal I help my clients achieve is bringing in consistent $5K months.

This goal needs to be specific, and a real, deep-seated desire. 'I feel like trying yoga' is not a customer goal, but 'I want to get fit and find a way to relax, so I might live until a ripe old age and not keel over in my thirties due to work-related stress' is. It's the motivation behind your customers spending with you.

If you're not sure, think about the questions you're often asked. What's the problem you tend to solve for your people? No woolly vague answers. People pay for specific measurable results, not for a general sense of wellbeing.

Step by Step

What are the big steps someone needs to take in order to reach that goal?

For example, the chapters in this book loosely represent the steps in my process.

Look for four to six big steps in your process. Are these the steps you've followed yourself in order to achieve your success? Are these the steps you'd work on with a client? Do they solve the main problems that someone has when you work with them? Is there a logical flow?

These steps, the things your people need to do in order to achieve their goal, are going to form the backbone of everything you do. They are the guts.

Marketing Magic

Time for a bit of marketing magic. We need to wrap your process up in a jazzy way so that it's more than just a list of a few things.

Give it a name, so we can refer to it. So that it comes to life and it becomes a product, not just a random bunch of thoughts. Come up with a catchy way to label each step in your process. For example, in my Profit Path (the name I've given my process), the steps are:

1. BIG VISION
2. BIG LOVE
3. BIG PACKAGE
4. BIG PERSONALITY
5. BIG PROFIT
6. BIG IMPACT!

The thing is, when you package your process like this, it becomes more than the sum of its parts. Whatever content you're selling, might not be revolutionary, or unique, but when it's wrapped up into something that sounds splendid, you will grab people's attention and they will pay for it. It convinces them that they're going to get results.

Different Formats

Once you have a framework sorted it's up to you how you use it. It can form the backbone of everything you do. From books, to courses, to planners, to programs—you name it. Let's run through some different options.

Group programs

The simplest way to leverage your time and expertise is to work with more than one person at the same time. If you create a group program then, instead of a handful of one-to-one clients, you can work with hundreds of people at once.

I love bringing people with a common goal together and working with them all at the same time. I feel like people get a lot out of being part of a group. The support and camaraderie adds another level to the work I can do.

You could run a group program over a limited time period to help people achieve a specific goal. You could use a Facebook group to bring people together. And you could have a weekly live coaching group call and a workbook to support them along the way.

You don't need much tech—only Facebook, a way to package content (PDF files for example), and a group email. It's really simple.

You could do this with anywhere from four people up to a few hundred, depending on your work.

A group package like this is live, and gets people face time with you, but it's also remote. No more travelling. No more being limited by distance or being restricted by the people in your local area.

It was a big step for me the first time I did this. I was really scared. So I understand that this might feel daunting to you too. But actually, if you start really small, it's easy. And you'll feel an amazing sense of possibility once you've done it, because it opens up the doors to your business really scaling up.

Don't worry about getting everything perfect. You could start off with a rough outline and then based on the needs and the feedback in the group, you could create the content as you go along. You could use it as a beta test to trial out content and then depending on how it goes you could turn the content into something more permanent afterwards.

I ran a live group coaching program like this—it was called Project Profit.

It was six weeks long with a specific outcome. It enabled me to work with 30 women at once, instead of just one at a time.

How could this model work in your business?

Products

A product is something that you create once and sell over and over again. If you run a service-based business you might not have any products. Not yet, anyway. But you can think creatively. A product could be an online course, an eBook, a planner, a how-to guide, membership, bundle of pre-prepared scripts or printables, a workbook, the video or transcription of an event you spoke at. A fitness instructor could sell a workout series or a weight loss planner. A stylist could create a style guide or a seasonal trend book.

What could you create once that lots of your customers could use themselves? Think about things that can replicate value; templates, cheat sheets, tools, diagnostic questionnaires, guides, planners, worksheets, videos, meal plans and mini courses.

If your product can be digital then this is ideal. We don't want to be going to the post office every day! You can sell a digital product on your website without having to do a thing.

If you do want to sell physical products, think of smart ways of doing this. For example, you could use a print on demand service like Blurb to distribute a book or workbook.

You may already have a ton of content that you could rework. Maybe you have a blog series from a while back, a talk you did, a podcast you made, that free eBook, a quiz you designed, a challenge you set people. Look at what you already have and see if you could turn it into something to sell.

Creating products is also a great way to build trust with customers, letting them get to know you before they invest in your high-end services. Once they've tried your course, bought your planner, read your book, taken your training series, they're more likely, assuming it was good, to want to work with you again, and take it to the next level.

Once you've created a range of entry-level products, they can be doing the work of wooing your people without you.

★ ★ ★ CASE STUDY: FIONA LATIF ★ ★ ★

Fiona Latif, is a hypnotherapist who loves empowering clients to move forward with positive changes in their lives. www.hypnobites.com

I was working full time in Financial Services when I started my part-time hypnotherapy practice. At first it was going really well as I was lucky enough to have clients through word of mouth, even before I got my website up and running. Clients were getting results and I was getting a lot of referrals.

But it quickly got to the point where all my spare time was devoted to seeing clients, or preparing for sessions. It was weekday evenings, weekends, then weekday mornings before work. I was getting one day off a month and that was usually spent catching up on sleep! I was starting to get burnt out.

The time I was spending per case was not sustainable or cost effective. I was breaking even, but only because, effectively, I wasn't charging for my time. With the cost of the therapy rooms there wasn't much left over at all! To be a viable business, I needed to find a method for treatment that was more efficient.

I love hypnotherapy, but my business had to work around my life. So I started to develop hypnobites.com and a series of tailored hypnotherapy recordings that people could download in their own time and in the comfort of their own home whilst still having the same impact. Essentially, I've turned my service into a product. My clients can now get access to the full treatment plans that I would normally offer all my face-to-face clients online, and at a better rate!

★ ★ ★

Hybrid model

My favorite product model is what I refer to as an Academy. It's a mixture of an online course, a membership site and a group program. Mine is called the Profit Pack; it's a small group of people united by a common goal, to achieve $5k months.

I find membership sites and online courses are too passive and don't always get the best results for people because they're left to their own devices. Clubs can often be way too big, and with thousands of members it's hard to get the support you need to really achieve your goals.

I love the Academy model because it can start small, with as few as 20 members, and can increase to around 200 members. It's easier to get started and the numbers are more achievable. You don't need a huge mailing list or to be incredibly well known to do this.

Members follow a structured program online that includes videos and workbooks. The structured content reduces my workload because I'm not answering the same questions over and over again. Content is drip fed a week at a time so that people can work at their own pace and don't get overwhelmed.

How to Make Your Products

Creating products is easy these days. We're so lucky. You don't need an agency or a production studio. We can shoot high-quality videos on our smartphones. We can self-publish books. There's software to host courses. It's all there. Honestly, what a time to be alive!

I create all my products myself. I occasionally hire a freelance editor to polish up my videos, but on the whole, my stuff is made by just me.

I have a few basic bits of equipment in my shoe-cupboard office. I shoot my videos using my phone. I create my PDFs in Powerpoint. And that's it really.

It's so easy to create stuff now that anyone can do it, but your products still need to be of a professional quality that reflects the value they offer.

Even if you're creating your own downloadable PDFs or shooting a video course in your spare bedroom, make sure you get someone to proofread your writing, brush up your design skills, set up good lighting and a professional looking background for your video. Plan your content before you create it. People need to be able to understand you, see you and hear you to get what you're on about.

★ ★ ★ CASE STUDY: JO SIMPSON ★ ★ ★
Jo Simpson helps female entrepreneurs grow their empires with her company Financial Growth Academy www.financialgrowthacademy.co.uk

I had been running a traditional professional services business for 15 years; I had a great team, business was good and some large clients on retainers meant we didn't have to worry about generating new business. But I felt trapped; restricted to my local area and tied to just another job. I was struggling to work out how to scale my business beyond the local.

I had to recognise that there was a whole world of people out there who needed my help to overcome their fear of finances, and that I needed to create something that would help more people at the same time. Something that could be scaled to generate recurring revenue, without taking up even more of my time. The Financial Growth Academy was born, an online platform, providing tools and resources to help entrepreneurs manage their finances. I still work one-on-one with clients, but I do it virtually, and I also sell a financial success course and a mastermind programme. Now I'm able to work with hundreds of entrepreneurs to help them better manage their finances and grow their businesses. I hadn't appreciated my experience was as valuable as it is!

Step by Step Along the Process

Don't just give people a whole bunch of information. In the past I've had a vault of information but people got overwhelmed and didn't really use it. Often when people are trying to achieve something, the reason they need help and haven't done it yet is that they're overwhelmed and they need someone to hold their hand. If you overload your people with information, they're going to feel even more overwhelmed and their progress may stall again.

Instead you want to drip feed the content a week or a month at a time. You can either do this in bundles each month with a theme, or you can do a step-by-step process that leads someone towards achieving a goal. Break it down for people. Make it clear where they are in the process so they can see their progress and where they're at.

Personal Contact Support and Accountability

Online courses have their pros and cons. From a business point of view they're great because you just sit back as people sign up for your stuff and you count your money. But you need to sell a load of them. And the results people get can be underwhelming, because they're having to self-motivate with no accountability.

The reason I love my Academy model is because I'm available to actually help people. We have group coaching calls where I can teach topics and people can ask me questions. This is so important- it's what makes it special.

Community

If you can build a sense of community through your products then you're on to something really powerful that will motivate people to buy more from you, at the same time as encouraging them to achieve their goals. In my Profit Pack academy, members have a sense of identity. We call ourselves the Profiteroles. We have a manifesto. We're united by a common aim. I'm a Profiterole and I'm going big! We have a common language. #lovingyourwork #squadpower. It makes us feel part of something, which is so important when you spend all day on your own.

For many of us, we feel like the people around us just don't get us. We tell them our latest mad idea and we're met with silence or a harrumph, or a shake of the head, as if we're some kind of nutter. But when the Profiteroles are in the Profit Pack, they're part of a gang, a gang of women who get them, who appreciate them and who are in the same boat.

It's the power of community. We all share a common goal and we help each other to get there. Real friendships are formed. This is powerful stuff, a glue that sticks together relationships and binds people to your brand.

Pricing

When you're launching a new product for a service business, it's tempting to price it low and aim for big numbers, especially if it's a membership model. We assume that getting a few hundred people in will be simple if we set a low price. But finding paying customers is a lot harder than it looks and involves a considerable investment in advertising to get there. It takes a long slog at a low price point to reach the place you need to be. So instead, spend that same time and budget on advertising but go in at a higher price point. Instead of aiming for a couple of hundred customers at $15 a month, an academy could charge $97 or $197 or $297 a month and only have to hit a few sales to get to the same point. Remember that you're charging for the value you are offering to customers—how much will they realistically pay to fulfil their deepest desires?

Real Impact

An Academy is an intimate way of offering a product to your customers. It enables you as the leader to really impact lives and create a transformation for your people, but you're reaching more of them at once. It works for people who can't afford your one-to-one rates but they still want a piece of you. They still get to be in your gang and get your help!

I love seeing the changes my Profit Packers make in their business. They launch programs, get more clients and make more money in their business. It makes me feel all warm and fuzzy!

Boundaries

Remember, a product like an Academy is not the same as offering a client one-to-one support. Yes, you love your people but you don't want everyone to come live with you! For this reason, it's crucial to set official boundaries on how much of yourself you give access to. If people start texting or messaging you at all hours, you'll soon want to run away from the whole thing.

Make it clear what's acceptable and what you're prepared to do. Maybe it's a once a week session with you live in a Facebook group, a regular phone call slot or a web chat, but whatever it is, it should be made clear from the start.

★ ★ ★ CASE STUDY: LAURA ROBINSON ★ ★ ★
Laura Robinson is digital copywriter and content strategist
www.worditude.co.uk

I'm good at what I do and I have a good reputation, so most of my work was coming through referrals. But the way I was structuring my business wasn't working. I was odd-job copywriting, living hand-to-mouth. My income would swing wildly from month after month. It was stressful. I didn't want to turn work down because I didn't know when the next job was coming from, but I'd end up overbooked. I was undercharging too, and I knew it, which was bad for motivation.

The question was, how could I make more money while reducing the stress and unpredictability of the work? I wasn't keen on simply raising my rates in order to earn more. I'm passionate about helping new businesses without a huge budget to throw at problems., but raising my rates would shut them out and attract an entirely different type of client, who could throw money at the problem but not engage with me.

So I came up with an alternative to higher rates; the Worditude Club. It's an online platform that offers affordable way for solopreneurs to work with a professional copywriter and content strategist (that's me by the way). Members can use the online library of workbooks and training materials to write their own web copy and blog posts, in their own voice, sprinkled with their own personality.

Now Worditude Club is making a fairly consistent income of £2000-£3000 each month and is growing nicely. Instead of constantly searching for the next paying job, I am receiving repeat income from a core of members I love to work with. And it's bringing in one-to-one work from clients who need a little extra support. I love the fact that I will never ever have a j-o-b ever again!

Price It Right

I used to struggle with pricing. I was living in a dark and dingy bargain bin; trapped in a cycle of over-delivering and undercharging, exacerbated by my ridiculous self-doubt and fear of rejection. Pitiful.

After I wrote my first book, I went on to launch a network for female entrepreneurs. On the outside it was huge, but the reality was, it didn't make much money at all. My money mindset issues saw to that.

Rationally, I knew my prices were too low, but I didn't have the confidence to match the competition. From a strategic point of view it was clear that the meet-ups I was offering were value-packed and provided amazing support for members. Where our competitors were charging meeting fees on top of a significant membership fee, I kept our prices super low, because I didn't want to come across as greedy, or upset anyone. My gremlins were doing a great job at keeping me small.

My reticence and awkwardness around money had consequences for the business, as much as I hate to admit it now. (But, we're friends now, right... I mean you know a lot about me by now.) People would haggle on price, skip payments pleading poverty, (having driven there in their Mercedes, wearing Laboutins) or forgetting to bring their money (to the bar. Who does that?!)

What a mess.

I knew I needed to scale the business so I introduced my first membership site, in the days before they were even really a thing. I did a lot of things right, but, stuck in my money mindset quagmire, I still felt like my pricing had to sit sullenly at the bottom of the barrel.

So, then, one summer weekend, I was in the countryside celebrating my dad's 60th birthday at a cool country house with my extended family and all his dad-like beardy friends.

I was sipping Pimms on the lawn, when my mobile rings, and I was like "Ello?!" shouting to be heard over the string quartet in my weekend off duty voice, because it was the weekend, I'd had a few drinks and wasn't really expecting a work call.

At the end of the fuzzy line, there was a narky voice. "I'm a student member of your network... and the thing is, I'm a bit strapped for cash this month, and I've changed my mind. I don't want to be a member any more, and you've just charged me $3 and I want my money back."

I was like, "Yeah sure you can have your $3 back!" I was cursing them inwardly to myself. Except that it wasn't anyone's fault, except my own.

I put the phone down. It was a massive light bulb moment for me. I felt like someone had just chucked a bucket of ice water over me. I'd just spent 20 minutes on the phone, on the weekend, when I was meant to be hanging with my fam, about a refund of $3! And to make matters worse, I would have to go into my system that very day and sort the refund, which would take another 10 minutes of my time. When my brother asked me what I was doing, I made something up about a PR opportunity because I was too ashamed to admit how ridiculous I was being.

Going to bed that night, I couldn't shake that feeling. Was I completely ridiculous? I was not running a business. I'd landed myself with an expensive hobby. I had to make some pretty significant changes if I was going to generate the kind of profits I dreamed of.

Pricing is like a window into your mind; it says a lot about how you're feeling about yourself and your abilities. Before you can sort your pricing out, you have to sort out the stuff going on in your head. But once you do, it's amazing. The quickest way to make more money in your business is to charge more money. Obvs.

In the years that have followed, I've been through massive pricing challenges and epiphanies. And, happy to say, I've finally sorted myself out. I still have a wobble every now and again, but over time, it's got a lot easier!

These days my pricing reflects the value I deliver and the impact I have on my clients' businesses and lives. And my pricing strategy allows me to run a sustainable business, so I can keep helping lots of people. (And buy nice things, too of course.)

Our Own Pay Gap

As entrepreneurs, we have the potential to generate as much revenue as we like. There is no ceiling. And yet, we're actually limiting our potential and creating our very own entrepreneurial gender pay gap. We are literally doing it to ourselves. And it has to stop.

Working with hundreds of female entrepreneurs over the years has opened my eyes. I know now why women continue to earn less than men, especially in their own small businesses. No matter the business— tech start-ups, dietician, copywriter, photographer, fitness instructor—

the common thread is that women often lack the confidence to charge their true worth.

Going in at a low rate is too often our default position. Add in price negotiations from the client and throwing in extra 'freebies' to sweeten the deal and we end up working all hours for tiny profits. What are we playing at?

We've waited a long time for the gender pay gap to close, and yet it persists. We entrepreneurs have the power to fix it! We owe it to ourselves, and to future generations.

Warning Signs Your Pricing Sucks

- You're not making any flippin' money!
- You're a lot cheaper than all your competitors. When you look at your competitors, do you come up with a whole bunch of reasons why you're cheaper than them? That's not good.
- You feel awkward setting prices in the first place. And when someone asks you the price, you mumble and make something up.
- You're exhausted because you're working all the hours but you're still not making any money.
- You seem to attract people with no money.
- When people aren't buying from you your immediate reaction is to slash your price.
- You worry that if you raise prices you'll lose clients.
- You've started to resent doing the work.

★ ★ ★ CASE STUDY: TRACY HOOPER ★ ★ ★
Tracy Hooper is an image consultant.
www.dorrieandflo.com

When I first started working with Nadia and she suggested I go online with my image consultancy business, I didn't think it was even possible! I mean, image is something that needs to be done with the person present... how on earth could it be possible without actually seeing the person in the flesh! But then we started looking at clients I could work with and niche things I could offer, and I began to see that it could work.

One of the things that required the biggest mindset shift for me was pricing. I thought I was charging a reasonable rate for my services. And who was I to think I could earn more than any of the other people in my industry, particularly when I believed they knew more than me?

But I slowly began to realise that if your pricing is too low people think you're providing a lower quality service. It was a revelation; people actually want to pay more, because it makes them feel like they're getting a higher level of service and they'll achieve better results.

So I have put my prices up. The first time I had to tell somebody what I now charged, I could hardly believe I heard myself saying the figures! But the very first potential client I spoke to came back to me, and said she was happy with the quote. I was blown away.

Now I know it's all about the value I'm delivering, not the number of hours I spend with them. The work I do makes a huge difference to the way my clients feel about themselves, their brand and their business.

When one of my clients goes into a meeting with a prospective client or supplier, they've actually done a lot of the hard work before they even have to speak, just by the way they look. I love that! That's what I'm selling, the outcome.

Perfect Pricing

Right, let's get to work. Together we're going to whip your pricing into shape.

Let's imagine your pricing strategy is like a cake. Right now it may resemble a shriveled-up sunken sponge. Rather than try to save it with icing, we're going to get a fresh bowl of ingredients and start from scratch, until your pricing resembles a plump and profitable work of art with a cherry on the top. Here's how.

Get over yourself

Stop being so self-obsessed! Pricing is not about you, your self-worth, how you look, how stylish you are or how shiny your website is. Time to get over ourselves. Even if you have created a personal brand and you're the one delivering the work, you're not actually selling yourself. Your pricing should be based on the value you're delivering to your people. It's about what they'll pay for the impact and the transformation that they will experience when the work with you.

Create a sustainable business

If you're cheap, you won't make enough money to survive. Unless you're propped up by a trust fund or a rich spinster auntie, you're going to eventually have to start spending your savings or rob a bank. Either way your business will crumple, and all the people you were put on this earth to help will be left hanging or will find someone else to help them. If you want to continue doing what you do best, for the long term, your business needs to be profitable.

Elevate your attitude

Think of yourself as a VIP when it comes to your time. It might feel strange, especially if you're a shy people-pleaser like me. Remember that one-on-one time with an expert (you), is worth a lot; it's the most exclusive way of working with you and should be priced accordingly. Don't just chuck your time at people willy-nilly. If you want your clients to respect your expertise, set your prices accordingly. If you're always available and your one-on-one work is barely differentiated from your group work or online programs, you're sending out a confused message and undermining your expertise.

Let go of guilt

If you love what you do, that's awesome. But you can still get paid properly to do it. In fact, creating a business that helps people, brings you joy and makes you lots of money is splendid. It's nothing to feel guilty about. We all know lots of people who work their butts off in jobs they don't like to scrape a living. But honestly, who said work had to be hard and stressful and exhausting? If you're loving it right now, that's fab. No more squishing your profits by pricing it low because you feel bad for charging for something you love doing.

Bigger, better results

When I invest in a personal trainer, I make sure I turn up to the classes, particularly if I've paid in advance. And if I've handed over that cash and gone to the trouble of turning up every week, I'm a lot less likely to stuff my face full of ice cream and donuts immediately afterwards. I'm invested. Because I'm spending the money and dedicating the time, I'm more determined to get results. And because of that, those results will happen!

When you're cheap, you're actually making it harder for your clients to get results. This sounds a bit bonkers, but it's true! If you want your people to put the work in and invest their time and energy, your price needs to reflect the level of investment. If you're cheap, people won't be committed and they won't get results.

How many times have you bought something cheap and then not used it? Like that bargain top lying at the bottom of your wardrobe with the tags still on it. Or the time you signed up for that discounted online course and you didn't even open the first email.

If you want your people to get results, if you really care about the impact you're having on their lives, your pricing needs to be high enough for them to feel it! If your clients have had to really think about working with you, the chances are they'll make more effort, take it more seriously. And they'll get better results.

Cheap and nasty
When you look at your competitors, how do you compare? If you find yourself coming up with a whole bunch of reasons why you should automatically be cheaper, I may actually need to come round to your place and shake you. If people are used to paying $2,000 for a program somewhere else, why the heck wouldn't they pay you that amount too? If you're the cheapest, what kind of message does that send?

Consider the kind of people you want to attract. Your pricing is part of your brand. If you have a luxury product with a luxury design and luxury messaging, your pricing needs to reflect that.

Imagine you're getting quotes in for some work on your house. You get five quotes. One of them is significantly lower than the others. What do you do? Go with the cheap one? Or do you suspect that there's something sub-standard and maybe a bit questionable about them? Yeah, me too. Don't be the cheap option.

Going in low is a big no-no
In a race to the bottom of the pricing pit, the only business that wins is the one at the very bottom. Being the fifth cheapest isn't a great place to be. And that's why going low is a no-no. Because where does it end? If you get embroiled in a pricing war you'll be forced to go in lower and lower and lower until you're basically paying people to work with you.

Avoid bargain hunters
Consider who you want to actually work with. Your ideal clients are not bargain hunters able to sniff out a deal from 100 meters. We want to

work with people who appreciate the value we deliver, not a bunch of rodents whose whiskers start twitching at the thought of ditching you for an even cheaper option.

Many of my clients find that their higher-end clients are more appreciative and more fun to work with, compared to people getting a bargain. Go cheaper and you'll still find someone kicking up a stink, even when you're offering something for free.

A reiki healer client of mine told me about the time someone came into her store complaining that her $5 crystals were too expensive, all the while holding a massive Starbucks coffee. She clearly had $5 to spend on coffee, but not on a precious keepsake.

Something about low pricing seems to attract pain-in-the-butt clients.

★ ★ ★   CASE STUDY: KEZIA HALL   ★ ★ ★
**Kezia Hall helps women heal their bodies
and become fat burning machines.
www.supernaturallyhealthy.org**

It's heartbreaking for me to admit, but I'd got to a point where my love for my business was dwindling and I even felt some brewing resentment towards clients. I was working so hard for the world's smallest pay check and wondering if I was ever going to make the big bucks. But I felt awkward about raising my prices because I help people get well for a living. I mean, everyone should be able to afford to get well, right?

I cared a lot about my clients, so I'd spend hours and hours researching everything and answering every email in huge detail. Boundaries? What, boundaries?

But I came to realize that higher pricing meant better results for clients, because people who invest money are truly invested in their transformation. And sure enough, people were happy to pay my new rates, and I've got super-dreamy clients I love working with! I now know that pricing is not personal, it not emotional, it's just numbers.

With my increased income I hired a virtual assistant and OMG it has saved my life. Seriously. I've been able to step out of my business and start a MSc in Nutrition Science which I have been dreaming of doing for years but couldn't afford or make time for. The growth in my business means I can pay for my course and actually find the time to work on it!

I now know that my strength and joy lie in working directly with my people, so I'm concentrating on my membership program and my one-to-one clients. This made a big difference to my revenue and has given me such peace of mind. And now I am ready to take that to the next level.

Set yourself apart

When you do what you do in your own special way, it doesn't matter how much it costs. People will pay you because they like you. And they want to work with YOU.

If you try to copy everyone else, you'll immediately invite comparisons. If you really ramp up the uniqueness of your personal brand, it sets you apart from everyone else. You'll attract your kind of people, who will want to work with you no matter what.

Make it profitable

Look at your costs. And be sure to cover them. With lots left over! Add up your costs and work out how much you would need to charge to break even on each transaction. Costs are not limited to your phone bill. Don't forget these costs:

- Acquiring each new client.
- Delivering the work.
- Day to day running costs
- Paying yourself! (Please don't forget this one)
- Tax

If this is your base, from there you can look at how much profit you want to make on each sale. That's the exciting bit. And from there you can set your prices.

Focus on impact

Imagine you were selling face cream. Would you say to potential customers, "Buy this pot, there's gunk in it. And there's a label on the pot." You wouldn't would you? Nope, you'd sell the results; the fact that if they use your face cream they're going to have flawless, dewy, glowing skin, more fun in their lives, more confidence, hotter relationships, (and a better looking boyfriend maybe). Now that's worth paying for, right?

When you're pricing up your products and services, think about the impact you're having on your clients' lives, the desire you're fulfilling, and the specific impact you're having on their health / fitness / business / happiness. That's the value. And that's what your price should be based on. When you're pricing your products and services always think about the outcome, not just the nuts and bolts.

Create flow in your business

Think about how your prices work together and how they increase as trust and commitment builds. The more people trust you, the more they're willing to spend money with you.

Remember that your lower priced offerings should involve less, or none, of your time. Whereas your prestigious high-end products and programs will involve more of you and your time and attention.

Take your customers on a journey one step at a time, with enough differentiation between different levels. If you're charging just a few more dollars for them to go live with you and hang out with you every day for six months, why the hell would they do the course?

Test it and tweak

Pricing is not an exact science. If only it were! So, if you're still not sure about your pricing, let's take a loose approach and test it. If it doesn't work you can tweak it, increasing it gradually. Simple as that.

It's better to start testing at a slightly low price point and then move up gradually, rather than starting high and going down, as dropping prices doesn't generate confidence. You could grandfather your early adopters at the lower rate; so if you were launching an academy, you might start at $97 a month, and then after a few weeks increase the price for new people to $127, and then, a few months later, increase it to $147 for new people. That way you're rewarding your founder members for getting in quick and you can see how the price affects uptake.

Feel comfortable

No matter how you price your products and services, you need to be able to sell them! If every time you say the price out loud, you get the shakes, we have a problem. Not only will your clients sense your hesitation and probably turn and run, but you'll look like a right loon.

Make sure you feel comfortable with your price. Nobody can really tell you what that price should be, not even me. It's up to you. But, I challenge you to push yourself a little out your knitted comfy zone of cushti-ness. As you're thinking, cool, that gives me the excuse to change nothing and carry on exactly as I was, consider this; putting up your prices even a little, means you're going to make more money in your business. And that's what you want, isn't it?

Stick to it

It happens to the best of us; we set a new, higher price and try it out for a while, then we get cold feet. We get a negative reaction or don't win a client for some reason, and we're immediately tempted to dive back behind our old prices or fling in some discounts. I'd like to pretend that this never happens to me, but I'd be lying my socks off. In fact, given half the chance I'd be slashing my prices, in scenes reminiscent of Poldark with a scythe (If you have no idea what I'm on about, do yourself a favor and Google it, you'll thank me later).

Hang on, I just need to recover my composure.

Right, what was I saying? Oh yes, if you find yourself wavering and discounting your price, set your pricing structure out in written form. Having a solid pricing strategy in place will you help avoid any temptation to lower them or throw in freebies when speaking with your client. Write your price down, on your website. Have your pricing on your sales call scripts. It's simple but effective.

Putting your price out there means you'll attract people who can afford you. When you discuss price with a prospective client, they're already primed and they don't go "Whaaaat?! I was expecting it to be $250! But it's $5000 you maniac!" as they faint on the floor. It's a waste of time having discovery calls with people who've got no money, so set out your prices publicly to weed them out.

Review regularly

Now that you've set your prices you can breathe a sigh of relief. For now. But that's not it forever! Your prices need to increase every few months. So, you're going to put a date in your diary to review them again in say, 6 months. Put in that date or you'll wimp out. Unless of course, you hire me as your coach, and then I'll force you (gently) to do it!

I want you to train your customers to understand that your prices increase regularly. Because every day you become more and more awesome and more and more expensive. You're constantly developing your skills, you've helped loads more people, you might win awards, get press coverage in an amazing publication, you might even have published a book, or received some testimonials. And as a result you can increase your prices, yeah!

★ ★ ★ CASE STUDY: KATHY ★ ★ ★
Kathy Webster, artist and illustrator at Dotty Dog Art.
www.dottydogart.co.uk

I loved my business and the work I was doing, but I wasn't making any money. I was so busy working all hours on commissions that I didn't see my family.

But I felt that because I loved doing what I was doing, I shouldn't charge people much money for it. So I just kept saying 'yes' to the commissions and charging very little money for them. I thought this was what running your own business was all about. I was very wrong.

And deep down, I worried that I wasn't worth it and my work wouldn't live up to people's expectations. I was new to the world of commissioned portraits; why would anyone take me seriously as a newbie on the block?

When Nadia asked why my prices weren't on my website and suggested that I doubled them (!) my tummy turned to jelly.

Putting my prices out there for everyone (including other artists!) to see sounded so scary, but it was also so obvious. If I was going to commission a portrait, I'd want to know how much it cost, without the hassle of having to contact the artist to ask. So why wasn't I doing this?

So I did it! I doubled my prices and put them on my website. It immediately eliminated a massive amount of admin, as I no longer had to spend a chunk of my day replying to price enquiries.

Then, as the price enquiries stopped, everything went scarily quiet. I initially saw a drop in people contacting me. I started to doubt myself. What if people thought I was greedy? But what was really happening was that I was weeding out people who wouldn't end up commissioning me and freeing up time to grow my biz in other ways. When I secured my first commission at my doubled prices I was completely blown away. And since then, the commissions have kept on coming, which is a massive confidence booster.

I have increased my prices a number of times since then. Every time it's scary, but every time it gets a little bit easier. I have shipped portraits all over the world now, and I feel hugely proud that people choose me to paint their dog portrait for them, when there are so many other portrait artists in the world.

Do The Robot

Robots are taking over the world. Isn't it time we got some robot action in our lives? I'm not saying we should replace our friends and lovers with automatons, because that would just be creepy. I'm talking about something a lot less sinister; automating elements of your business, to save you time and money.

When it's just you in your business, you only have so many hours in the day available to you. And if you're anything like me, you also have a whole bunch of other responsibilities on your plate that require your attention. It's crazy, the amount of stuff we have to think about.

If time is of the essence, then doing every single thing manually in your business is not gonna cut it.

The numbers don't lie.

Let's assume you have 40 hours a week available to you, but in reality, you only want to work say, 20 hours a week, because you want to actually have a life and the whole reason you started a business was to have more fun, see your friends, and spend more time with your family.

What then? You probably have a whole bunch of stuff you need to do to keep your business running, so you only have around 10 hours you can actually bill each week.

If you were to sell every hour of your working time for $50 an hour—that's not much money, is it? Only $500 a week. $2000 a month. Dammit.

But what if you could bill 20 of those hours? You'd immediately boost your income potential to $1000 a week, or $4000 a month.

We're going to look at automating specific elements of your business to reduce the number of hours you spend doing some stuff, so you can focus on the stuff you do best, the stuff that only you can do, the stuff that makes you money.

I'm not recommending running your entire business on autopilot. You still need to be involved. You're the leader, the inspirer, the face of your business and people want to connect with you. I'm certainly not advocating your business becomes a faceless machine, because business is about people helping people. But robots help us leverage the time and resources we have available to us so that we can stretch them as far as we can, enabling us to grow our businesses as big as we possibly can without it getting any more complicated. With robots on our side, I'm happy to say, growing a business doesn't need to be a hellish, hassle-filled hustle. Automation makes it possible to turn your tiny business into a little big business that punches above its weight.

I love the idea that we can be just one person in our business and be running this huge machine. We're the face of our business, connecting with our people and then behind the scenes it's a tight ship, leveraging our time and expertise so we can reach thousands and thousands of people without even leaving the comfort of our home.

The Work

In your business, there are things that only you can do. This is THE WORK, the bit where the magic happens, and where you need to be focusing your time. This is your zone of genius.

Only you can deliver THE WORK, your signature service, whether that's photography, style advice, coaching, or nutritional advice. In addition, only you can record a video, do a livestream, write a book, give a talk, record a podcast, be photographed for a magazine, create content for your signature course.

Your focus needs to be here, because it's THE WORK that gets you paid. Our goal is for you to be able to automate the other stuff so you can focus your efforts here. After all, this is why you created your business in the first place; to do the work that you're passionate about.

The other stuff

The problem is, when you're running a business there's a whole bunch of other stuff that we need to do. Things like sending invoices, answering queries, scheduling calls, chasing payments ... yawn. This is the stuff that takes up our time, frustrating us and holding us back from being in the zone. It's also the stuff that many of us don't enjoy or feel we're not good at.

If you're a creative kind of a kid, chances are all the little details and processes associated with actually running a business get in the way, irritate you and bring you down.

Where to start?

Over the past few years, hundreds of software tools have popped up on the market, all with the intention of helping us to be more efficient and grow our businesses. There is a veritable smorgasbord of options, so much so that it can be rather overwhelming, if you don't know what you're looking for.

No matter what you do or how you do it, there are tools you can use to make your business more profitable and work harder for you, so you don't have to.

Don't rush into signing up for loads of tools until you've thought things through though. It's worth spending a few hours planning and thinking about your processes first. Try to identify the tasks that are gobbling up your time, the things you're terrible at, and the things you honestly can't stand.

Then we can see how the robots might be able to help.

★ ★ ★ CASE STUDY: NATALIE SILVERMAN ★ ★ ★
**Natalie Silverman is voiceover artist,
podcast host and radio presenter.
www.natchatproductions.com**

As a voiceover in a saturated market it is difficult to make yourself stand out when you are ultimately a voice being picked by someone else, plus I work part-time hours so it's important for me to have good systems in place in my business. That's why it's so important for my website to work really hard for me. Recently, I took my head out of the sand and had a proper look at what I was doing and how I could improve it. Once I'd made some changes to automate some of my sales processes, my business improved!

I've invested in a social media engagement tool, which makes it easier for me to become more consistent by scheduling content in advance. I use CRM to manage my customer relationships, which makes it easier for me to track leads, close deals and drive repeat business. I've also developed email templates to increase my productivity when targeting potential clients. Next up, I'm building automated email funnels to make my online marketing run like clockwork. And I'm going to start using Facebook ads for my voiceover business to sell packages and work harder on my online profile amongst my industry peers.

I now feel proud of my website and update my online voiceover portfolio regularly with the latest demos showcasing my work.

Get in touch

Imagine having a robot receptionist handling your enquiries and scheduling for you. Sounds good doesn't it? The good news is, if you have a website, you already do!

Don't neglect your website and leave it languishing like a sunbathing sloth. With a few clever tweaks, your website robot receptionist will go from comatose to cracking in no time.

First up, make sure your website explains clearly what your business is about and what you actually do. I know this sounds ridiculously obvious, but you'd be surprised as the number of site I've seen over the years that are confusing, vague and convoluted about what the business actually *does*.

Make it easy for people to get in touch with you. They shouldn't need to guess or spend ten minutes randomly searching your site to find your contact details.

Use prominent social media buttons so people can hook up with you easily online. Make it clear and easy for people to choose how to find our more and how to get in touch.

Your website should be set up with a goal in mind. What do you want people to do when they come into contact with you? Do you want them to sign up for your mailing list? Or do you want them to book in for a call? This is known as the 'action' you want people to take when they arrive on your site, and prompting them to actually do it is called a 'call to action'—for example, a nice big green button that says "Book a call." Whatever your goal, make what you want people to do, clearer than a pint of vodka. The clearer it is, the more likely it is to actually happen.

Get in the diary

An online scheduling system, will save you a ton of time messing around discussing availability and booking time slots with clients. This was one of the first tools I set up and it's been a godsend.

No more endless emails and messages about my availability spread over a week, ending in me pulling out my, already very short, hair when they finally settle on a date only to find someone has just booked it. Arghhhh!

It might seem like stuff like this will only save you minutes, but all those minutes add up to valuable hours and hours over the course of a year. Software such as Acuity or Calendly may not be free, but it's a heck of a lot cheaper than paying a real-life person to manage bookings.

When someone books in for a breakthrough call with me, they have a series of qualifying questions to answer. I ask them about their business goals, whether they've worked with a coach before, whether they've got a clear idea of what they're looking for, and importantly, what their budget is.

This is all done automatically and means that I'm able to pre-screen people before I speak to them. No more wasting time talking to people who fancy a chat and have no intention of working with me. It might sound harsh, but your business won't grow if you're spending hours on the phone talking to people who are not right for you.

Get booked

Are you making it hard for people to pay you?

I used to have a personal trainer who made it ridiculously difficult to pay him. It had to be via bank transfer, every five sessions, but neither of us could ever remember how many sessions I'd had. I had to keep track in my diary, so I wouldn't forget to pay him. And he didn't do receipts or reminders. And it was up to me to go into my bank and make the transfer manually. Eugh. So much hassle. He was a great trainer, but in the end I couldn't take it anymore and went elsewhere. Working with him was causing me the wrong kind of pain!

If you're sending manual reminders, tracking payments on paper, carrying around cash, forgetting to take money on the day, and generally not having a clue who's paid what, it's time to get a grip! It's bad for your cash flow, but equally importantly it's terrible for customers; if you forget stuff or you lose paperwork or you're slow to respond then you're not giving your people the best experience. They will go elsewhere!

If people want to pay you online but, because you have no idea how to take online payments, you send them an invoice and they have to go into their bank and set up a transfer, you're probably really pissing them off.

Imagine how cool it would be if all that was streamlined. Your email comes through and they click on it. And boom, all paid.

You can also link up invoicing with contracts and waivers, so that as people are paying, they can also sign the paperwork and book in for sessions, all online, all without you having to lift a finger. Plus, you'll be able to easily track who's paid what and when. Genius!

There are some great pieces of software that will enable your clients to do all this online. Head over to Capterra.com where you'll easily find the right solution for you and your business.

Get answers

If you're living in your own personal Groundhog Day, answering the same questions from potential clients over and over again, eventually you'll start to feel like a robot yourself. If you're drowning in questions, it's time to take control.

The first step is simple; create an FAQs page on your website, answering all the questions one at a time, in a logical order. Then, when someone gets in touch, you can direct them to that page. You could also save your email responses in a document, so you can cut and paste. That would save you some time.

If you're after something a little more snazzy, why not create your own helpdesk? A tool like Zendesk enables you to have live chat on your site with a ticketing system that makes it easy to keep track of all your enquiries, as well as pre-prepared answers to the most common questions about refunds, delivery, timings and so on.

If you're selling a complex, or high-ticket product, and you feel like people come to your sales page and leave again with questions still hanging, this kind of service could help increase your conversion rate by making sure people don't get confused and wander off without making a purchase.

Get paid

There are some excellent money management systems out there which make it easy for you to manage invoices, purchase orders, accounts and more. Most even do a lot of the donkey work for you. If you haven't already got something set up, what are you waiting for?

Get organized

I like listening in on people's conversations, especially in cafés when I'm supposed to be working. Here's an approximate version of something I heard this morning:

"The business is growing, but it's so hard to control. I've got lists of lists, and you know how I feel about spreadsheets. Last week I rang a potential client, only to find I'd rung them yesterday." Cue, much flustered arm waving, a latte spillage and one rather soggy diary. There were almost tears. And that was just me.

Reluctant to reveal my true earwigging colors, I had to restrain myself from interrupting and mentioning that a customer relationship management system (CRM) could help reduce the chaos and avoid future disasters.

A CRM is like an address book on steroids. Its purpose is to help you manage and nurture customer relationships. It's usually a cloud-based system that stores information about your clients, potential clients and contacts in one central place. A CRM can also help you grow your business and keep customers happy by keeping track of interactions and tasks, giving you a clear view of your sales pipeline.

As your business grows, so will the amount of client data you need to manage. Instead of relying on lots of different lists and spreadsheets, sticky notes and the back of your hand, a CRM will keep all your client info in one easily accessible place. No more mistakes, missing files, omissions or unnecessary repetition.

Trying to remember everyone's contact details as well as who spoke to who, when and why, will drive you to distraction. Don't waste your brain power on this stuff; put a CRM system in place, so you can focus on greater things.

Your business is built around strong client relationships. Forgetting to call or follow up is a bit rubbish really. A CRM will help you remember key actions, resolve potential issues before they get out of hand, and help you deliver a great service.

Plus, your CRM will help streamline your sales process. You'll know where each lead is at so you can focus your efforts accordingly until you close the deal. Then, when someone signs up, you can automatically send intake questionnaires, guides and other useful bits, automatically.

Information stored in a cloud-based CRM will be kept safe from drooling dogs, small children and cups of tea, as well as team members who tend to leave laptops on trains.

If you're forever sending the same emails again and again, a canny CRM system will be able to automate workflows for you so you can nurture leads, welcome new clients, add value through automated training and manage your team without lifting a finger. Boom.

Keeping track of emails and conversations with your contacts could prove useful, if you ever face a difficult situation, or even a legal dispute. Having a clear record to hand of all your interactions by client could help sort out any problems before they arise, let alone escalate.

You might think software like this costs a bomb, and in some cases you'd be right. But the good news is that there are some great products out there starting at free or at just a few dollars per month such as Airtable, Insightly, Capsule, 17hats, and Zoho, all of which are simple to use, and do not require a computer science degree.

Get connected

Building a list of your peeps and emailing them regularly is the simplest way to build relationships and sell to people.

I'm not completely obsessed by automated funnels, because I do like to email people when inspiration strikes, but there's a lot of value in automating some emails. For example, when someone signs up to my list, or registers for an event, or signs up for a freebie, they get an automated series of messages designed to build trust and invite them to connect with me.

I love the fact that I can wake up in the morning to a bunch of scheduled calls, and even some sales. That's a great feeling. Making money while you're sleeping!

Rather that go in for the hard sell, I use email marketing to help me warm people up so that they get to know me and like me and trust me, without my having to do any work at all. It makes selling a whole lot easier because people are ready to buy.

When you're setting up your email funnels, don't get carried away and start pounding people to buy from you right then and there. Remember, there's a real person at the end of the email you're about to write. Talk to them like you're talking to a friend. Think about how they might be feeling and what they need to hear from you in order to trust you and ultimately fall in love with you, so they're ready to spend all their hard earned cash on you.

Get seen

I'm all about minimum effort maximum impact. And that's why I harness the power of video and Facebook ads to create a marketing machine that drives my business forward with the minimum amount of effort on my behalf.

I start off by creating video content that my kind of people find engaging. This could be just one good video a month of me sharing business tips. And then I drive eyeballs to that video using Facebook ads. I make sure there's a strong call to action in the video and in the accompanying text so that the video is growing my audience and also my list.

Once I have an ad that works well, I'm able to turn it on and off when I need it. This system makes it easy for me to connect with thousands of potential clients. And although it does cost money, it's brilliantly targeted and outcome-oriented so that I only pay for actual conversions—in my case, sign ups to my list or registrations for a webinar or training.

Get learning

If you've ever considered creating an online course, an academy, membership or group program, you've probably wondered how to deliver the materials to your participants. And that's where a learning management system comes in.

My Profit Pack works on autopilot. I add content and videos and they are drip-fed to my members. I know that when someone signs up and pays, they'll get access to the materials, one week at a time. My job is to create the materials and be there for my people; I don't have to worry about sending stuff out.

I use a learning management tool called Thinkific which I love, but there are lots of alternatives too which will save you a bunch of time and create a smooth and professional learning experience for your members.

Get printed

I love this one! I use print-on-demand tech to distribute my Pure Profit Planner and a range of other merch for my people. When someone buys, the product is printed and shipped, all without me doing a single thing. How cool is that?! Check out Blurb for books, Spreadshirt, Redbubble and Printful for other items from t-shirts to mugs and bags. I love how simple it all is, and that you don't need to fill your house with boxes or even go to the post office. The wonders of modern technology, eh.

★ ★ ★ CASE STUDY: NIKI STEPHENSON ★ ★ ★
**Niki Stephenson is an online marketer
for helpers, healers and creatives.
www.computerbluemedia.co**

Business was booming, but I was overwhelmed, overstretched and on the verge of a crash-and-burn. I was having to turn clients away. It was crazy.

My head virtually exploded when Nadia helped me to see that there was a completely different way to provide a service for people, that didn't involve trading hours for dollars.

Before, I'd been on an endless hamster wheel of uploading content to social media for various clients, so I redesigned my social media packages to make them more automated and free up my time. Even better, I figured out I could automate the invoicing and set up monthly recurring autopayments for these packages, so I never had to wonder when I'd get paid next!

Making these changes was a massive confidence-builder, and I was able to strike a better balance at home and actually spend time with my family, not just my computer screen. Automation allowed me to have a life outside of work.

A word of caution

You may not need to use all these tools in your business, but I'm pretty sure that some of them will help you to be more efficient and focus on the stuff you do best. I get that you will have to spend a little to use some of these, but in comparison with the cost of hiring someone to do these jobs manually, it's a heck of a lot cheaper.

Beware, there are loads of options and there are some very shiny things out there. Please don't lose the plot and sign up for all the things! Make sure the different pieces of software integrate with each other, and be sure to make the most of free trials to see if you get on with it before you commit.

It may not be possible to have one system that does everything. I've tried. It might be that you need a few things that integrate together. Better to choose something that does what you need brilliantly and have a few things linking together, than have one system that doesn't do what you need.

Squad Power

Let It Go!

Let me start this chapter by telling you that I am a massive control freak. (Pretty sure I get it from my mother, but don't tell her I said that). I like being the boss of my business and I like working on my own. After I had a bad experience with a previous business partner and my business dissolved into the ground, I vowed that from then on I would be a lone ranger. And on the whole, I like it that way.

But that doesn't mean I work completely alone. There is no way I could have grown my business without getting help. Trying to do everything, every single flipping thing, will kill your business, or at the very least chop off a limb or two.

How can you focus on growing your business if you're busy stuffing envelopes and doing the filing? Er... with difficulty. Your job as the founder is to focus on generating income and growth. You have to focus on the big stuff, and the things that you do best; your zone of genius. Just think how much extra money you could make if you weren't wasting time on things you struggle with, or little tiny things that take ages.

The DIY approach will kill you in the end. Just take Sally and her dog-sitting business. She came to me because she couldn't get past doing it all herself. She was taking on every single dog sitting job and spending her whole life sitting in other people's houses with other people's dogs. She didn't have any more days in the year left. And she couldn't chop herself in half or even quarters. The business was stuck.

But you know, I like a challenge. So Sally and I are working on new ways to grow her business, looking at how she can outsource tasks and identifying new sources of revenue that work around her life and her ambitions.

There's only one you in your business. And you only have so many fingers and toes and hours in the day. You only have a certain amount of time available to you. And if, like me, you don't work all day long, you're severely limited.

Refusing to get help is stunting the growth of your business. It can feel counterintuitive to spend money when your business isn't making loads of money yet. But the real question is, can you afford not to?

Outsourcing is not just for big business. Nowadays, almost any task can be outsourced to contractors. I love the fact that I can have a team made up of awesome people living all over the world. Hiring is now super simple thanks to the user-friendly platforms out there. And more and more people are sticking it to the man and working independently as freelancers and contractors, so the talent pool is huge.

That pool is waiting for you to jump into it; there are virtual assistants, copywriters, designers, bookkeepers, transcriptionists, web designers, IT gurus and PR consultants, just to name a few. By working with freelancers and contractors you don't need to get involved in the complexities of payroll and you can hire people as and when you need them. That global talent pool makes it possible for even the smallest business to compete with the big boys.

And yet we still resist

I used to think I could do it all. I thought I was the only one who could get stuff done in my business because I'm just that good. But over the years, as I've honed my skills, I've realized that I'm actually not the best person to do all the things. I'm owning my lack of expertise.

It may be hard to believe, because although I am rather splendid (!) I'm not the best at everything. In fact, I'm quite terrible at lots of things; bookkeeping, Facebook ads, and project management to name but a few. But in some ways being terrible at stuff is a good thing, because you'll be less tempted to have a go.

It's the things that you're not OK at that really suck your focus away from where it should be. I'm not bad at designing stuff; I do a pretty good job and I like the results. But it's not the best use of my time, because it takes me lots of time to do, time that I could be using to do other things. I'm much better off getting a proper designer to help me.

I get that letting go and getting help can be scary. I was worried that people wouldn't be able to do things the way I like them. That it would be quicker for me to do it myself. Or that I might as well just do it, rather than wait for someone to do it for me. Oh, and then there's the worry that someone might do a runner and nick all my stuff. And then of course there's the fact that it can be expensive to pay someone to help you. I get it. I do. And I get that it might feel odd at first. But you'll get used to it. And there will be no looking back! Done correctly, it will be the best money you ever spend and your business will love you for it.

It starts at home

We all have a lot going on in our lives. It's a wonder we have time to run a business at all.

If you're working from home, it makes it so much more tempting to roll up your sleeves and get involved with the house stuff, particularly when you have a low mess-threshold and people you live with have confused the floor with the wardrobe.

But just because you work from home and sit next to all that stuff that needs doing, doesn't mean you should be in charge of doing it all, at the same time as working. It's time for us to take a stand and start offloading some of this stuff. Do you really need to be the one doing all the house cleaning, ironing, picking up stuff, laundry, schlepping kids from activity to activity? And why isn't anyone else helping you? (Now that's an interesting question!)

The first thing we should be outsourcing is some of that goddamn house work. It's hard to build a business when you've got your head in the washing machine and your hands inside a pair of rubber gloves. Don't be a martyr. Trying to do it all is not big or clever and I'm fairly sure nobody will care, or even notice your efforts. Go get some help, for goodness sake.

My power team

In my business I have a virtual squad of highly skilled people. They're spread all over the world and I bring them in as and when I need them. They are all amazing at what they do; much better than me! And without them my business would still be tiny.

Jessica is my VA and she helps me with all kinds of admin, payment stuff and tech things. I do know how to do some of this stuff, but things that take me all day Jess can tick off in a few minutes. I'm a much nicer person to be around when I'm not grappling with tech.

When I'm in the flow or I'm booked up with clients the last thing I want to do is to stop to resend a lost invoice, or dig out someone's affiliate code, or find out why access isn't working. And that's why I have Jess.

Caroline is my Facebook ads guru. I find creating and monitoring ads time consuming and very technical. It's not my thing at all. I like seeing the results, but I'm not interested in fiddling around to get them. Which is why I have Caroline to help me!

I have no idea how to edit my videos, so I am more than happy to pay Herman to help me.

I hate bookkeeping. But I love the fact that Jo and her team do it for me, and they do it brilliantly and present me with a report at the end of each month. They probably also stop me making mistakes and ending up in jail!

I don't know what I'd do without these guys.

Things I definitely don't outsource

I've met people who plan to outsource everything. They see their business as some sort of pyramid scheme with them at the top sitting by a pool sipping cocktails. This isn't my style. Sure, automate stuff, hire people and put systems in place, but there are things you really need to be doing yourself. Don't take it too far. You are the heart of your business and your people need you.

For example, I don't believe I could ever outsource my coaching work to other coaches. People pay to work with me, so it would just be odd if they got someone else. I could grow a team of associates I guess, but it doesn't really appeal to me.

I'm also yet to be convinced that hiring a sales team is the way to go. I hate it as a potential client when I end up speaking to a sales person rather than the person I want to work with. How can I make a decision if I've never spoken to them? I remember one time I rang up about a program I was interested in joining and spoke to an amazing woman; she was funny and feisty and we really clicked. I signed up on the spot. But when I actually got started there was a different woman running it who was as dull as a pair of grey granny knickers.

I'm also not keen to outsource content creation. I love writing my programs and infusing them with my style. I don't think anyone else could do it just the way I do. And ultimately this is the stuff that people are paying for. I can get someone to format my PDFs, edit the videos and upload it to my website, but the actual content, that's my bag.

These things are the core of my business. They might be different from the core of your business, and you might make the decision to farm some of these out while keeping other elements for yourself; it all depends on what value you're offering and your own personal style. The key is to leave enough of yourself available to forge an authentic connection with your people.

★ ★ ★ CASE STUDY: MISS JADE MOON ★ ★ ★
Miss Jade Moon is founder of STEAMED, an edtech platform supporting young digital entrepreneurs.
www.missjademoon.com

One of my biggest turnarounds was employing a virtual team so that I could ditch simple and repetitive tasks. It gave me the freedom to create my new business and develop my clients. I've learned that it's totally impossible to do everything yourself. You need to invest in yourself, experts and outsource to succeed. I'm juggling lots of balls—a virtual team is the only way to keep them in the air!

The last year has been both tough and awesome. I went from zero to $10k a month in eight months and now I'm super excited about a second business I'm starting. And as a bonus, employing a team means I no longer feel alone in my work, plus I have more downtime in my personal life.

What Not to Do

On the whole, I've been lucky with the members of my virtual team. I've worked with some incredible people and they've helped me a lot. It hasn't always been that way though.

The first time I hired a virtual assistant, (let's call her Melinda) things took a very surprising turn.

I met Melinda in a Facebook group for entrepreneurs, where she seemed to be well respected and was working with a number of other members in the group. We got on like a house on fire and bonded over our sense of humour and the fact that we both had sons of the same age. Although we never met, we did lots of video calls and I felt like we were not only business buddies, but real friends too. I trusted her completely. I paid up front each month for the hours in our agreement. And we even arranged to attend a business event together, sharing a room.

And then, one day, she vanished. With my money. And not having done the work I asked her to do.

At first I was worried that something terrible had happened to her. I called friends who lived near her and asked them to go see if she was OK. I even called the police because I was worried that maybe she had had an accident.

But then as the weeks passed, and I didn't hear anything, I started to realise the scale of the scam. She had seemingly fallen off the face of the planet with a chunk of my money, and a chunk of lots of other people's money too and not delivered any of the work.

On further investigation, it turned out she was actually a criminal. She'd done this kind of thing before, lots of times and had even been to prison!

We just didn't see it coming.

You can't completely protect yourself from coming into contact with unscrupulous people in business, but you sure as hell can do more to protect yourself than I did. Did I get references for Melinda? Did I do a police check? Or even just Google her name before I hired her? Nope, I didn't. I just liked her, so I handed over the cash.

I won't be doing that again!

Top tips on hiring freelancers

Since then, I've got a lot savvier when it comes to hiring people. I get to work with some truly incredible people. And yet, for many people that is not always the case. Here are my top tips to help you get fantastic results from your virtual team.

- Meet people face to face, even if it's over Skype.
- Get really clear on what you want from them before you start.
- Write a brief with very clear instructions. People can't read your mind.
- Pay people properly if you want to get good results. Going for the bargain bin end of the virtual market will get you bargain bin quality.
- Plan ahead and don't expect to get everything delivered in five minutes. Good people tend to be busy and you may need to book in advance.
- Create a simple contract between you and any contractor you use.
- Pay when work is delivered. Don't pay up front unless you have to.
- Use platforms where money is held in escrow until work has been delivered.

- If there's an issue with delivered work, look at the instructions you gave. Chances are they weren't clear enough.
- Check references and reviews before hiring.
- Get off their back. Allow them to get on with doing their job. Nobody likes working with someone breathing down their neck.
- Be patient if there are language barriers and time zone differences.
- Only give out the absolute minimum data necessary for someone to do their work. Be mindful of keeping your data secure.
- Don't be a dick! Treat people nicely and with respect.

How to Get Unstuck

I used to be convinced I could manage my business on my own. No matter what went wrong, I'd soldier on, determined to prove everyone wrong. It never occurred to me to ask for help with business strategy. On the odd occasion I'd mention my business to a friend or family member, the response I'd get was never what I was looking for. Maybe they didn't understand what I was on about. Maybe they weren't really listening. Maybe their suggestions just weren't what I wanted to hear.

But I did need help. Not just help with the day to day stuff, but help with working out what to do, which direction to take my business. I knew it had potential but I couldn't quite decide on a business model that would allow me to scale. I kept switching between pricing structures and formats. It was all rather chaotic.

On the face of it I was successful. Published author. Business founder. I'd created something with huge potential. My beautiful, bouncy, business baby. I was passionate about it. I got to help hundreds, if not, thousands of women grow their businesses.

But it just wasn't paying the bills. And I couldn't figure out what to do. I was so close to it. So entrenched in the details, that I'd lost the bigger picture.

The irony was that I was great at giving other people advice and helping them with their businesses, but the idea that I'd hire someone to give me advice seemed a sign of weakness, so I would muddle on, going round in circles. The sense of overwhelm deepened.

Looking back, I wish I'd known what I know now. I wish I'd been strong enough to ask for help before I walked away. I wish I'd seen the value in paying for help, instead of telling myself I couldn't afford it. When actually I couldn't afford NOT to get help.

Unable to see a way forward and ready for a change, I folded the business and started again.

And this time around I hired a coach! The impact has been incredible. I've experienced first hand the power of a fresh perspective and the support of someone who has experienced what you're trying to achieve.

Don't make the same mistakes I made all those years ago. Don't be stubborn like I was. Don't be too proud to admit you need help. Don't keep banging your head against the wall, all on your own. Yes, you're a solo business owner, but you're not alone.

How a Business Coach Can Help

Hiring a coach was the best thing I ever did. Working with someone who is focused on my success. A sounding board. Someone whose sole purpose is to help me grow my business and move from where I am now to where I really want to get to.

When people around you are not necessarily supportive or understanding or even the slightest bit interested in what you're doing, a coach can be the person you need to bounce ideas off and give you feedback.

If you've got your head so buried in the day-to-day running of your business, it's hard to know which way to turn. Rather than wasting ages chopping and changing, there's a lot of value in getting an outside view from someone who's been there, who's done it, and is now where you want to be.

Coaching sessions are time for you to focus on nothing else other than you and your business. In my work I'm focused on everyone else's business, but when I work with my coach, I'm just focused on me. And in that time you've got accountability; someone to keep you on track, stopping you from getting distracted.

Pushing yourself out of your comfort zone is not easy. I know that, on my own, I wouldn't have launched a podcast, given talks to hundreds of people, raised my prices, or even written this book. These are all things I was clearly capable of doing, but I would never have done them without someone to give me a gentle (ish) nudge and support me in taking my business to the next level.

If you'd like to book a breakthrough call with me to discuss how I can help you take your business to the next level, head over to: www.nadiafiner.com/call

★ ★ ★ CASE STUDY: GEORGIE SNAPE ★ ★ ★
Georgie Snape helps adventure-seeking travellers relocate to Vietnam to teach English.
www.teach-vietnam.com

I knew I had something amazing, I just didn't have the right formula. I didn't have the expertise or knowledge to push it in the direction it needed to go. I felt lost because I wasn't sure how to progress. I loved my business concept but felt overwhelmed, alone, pressured and stressed that I was going to make a mistake. So I paid for business coaching with Nadia. I've gone from having weekly breakdowns and feeling in over my head, to knowing exactly where I'm at, what I want and how to get there. It won't all be easy, but I know I can handle it.

It made me realize that being me is the biggest strength in my business. You have no idea how much realising this has CHANGED EVERYTHING! Nowadays I feel a lot calmer about my business. I've noticed that I am talking about my business in a completely different, very positive way. This is what I'm going to do. It is not a hobby anymore.

The first thing in your budget should be business coaching. The rest will follow. The hardest thing about being an entrepreneur is doing it alone, so get help!

Your Squad

Motivational speaker Jim Rohn said that we are the average of the five people we spend the most time with. So who are you hanging out with? There's a lot to be said for having a squad of supportive business buddies with whom you can share your journey, goals and aspirations.

This may sound harsh, but if there are people around you dragging you down, it may be time to spend a little (or a lot) less time with them.

That's one of the things I love about my Profit Pack. The power of positivity is immense. Together we're all pushing each other to think bigger and aim higher, bit by bit. When you achieve something we're there to celebrate with you. And if you hit a low point, there's a whole pack of people helping pick you back up. Collaborations happen, partnerships are formed. And there's the joy of helping others out.

Don't try to ride the wiggly wave of entrepreneurship all by yourself. Surround yourself with people who believe in you, people who support you and inspire you to go big.

★ ★ ★ CASE STUDY: MUIR DE GUZMAN CHAVEZ ★ ★ ★
**Muir de Guzman Chavez, helps sprouting
entrepreneurs with clarity and strategy.
www.MuirChavez.com**

I don't just go giving out my energy all willy-nilly to anyone. And I keep those that feel the same very close.

Sometimes, once you start to come into your own and experience any kind of success, you lose those that you once thought would be in your life forever.

But in my experience, the universe will never leave you alone for too long. Those empty spaces fill quite quickly with humans that are equal or greater in that powerful energy that is needed to survive this rollercoaster of being an entrepreneur. I have lost many and gained many.

While some are available in my everyday life, others may be on another continent. Some I have met in person. Others I have never met, and yet I can jump on a video chat with them at 3am and they will be there for me. This is the kind of energy that you NEED to surround yourself with.

BIG
IMPACT

Sweat Free Sales

I've always got a buzz from spreading the word about businesses I rate. I'm a connector. It makes me happy to do it because I know I'm helping both the business and the person who needs help. And maybe, in a strange way, it makes me feel powerful or something. In any given day I probably recommend around ten different things to my mates and my tribe. It's why I was great at running a PR business, because I got paid to do it!

But if it's so easy to sell other people's services, why is it so freakin' hard to sell yourself?! Even when you're promoting a product, a sales fail can feel like a personal rejection, and it's worse if promoting your business basically means promoting yourself, because your business is you. It can feel a tad uncomfortable. OK more than a tad, a total tad.

Many of us approach sales with reticence and fear. We're afraid of getting a no. It's like walking up to someone in a bar and inviting them on a date. What if they say, no thanks, you're not my type? Or something worse? Not nice. And because we're afraid of personal rejection, and therefore afraid of selling, we just don't do it.

I get it. I sometimes feel funny about selling too. When friends tell me they've watched one of my videos with a call to action at the end, I get a bit freaked out. But when I became a coach and created a personal brand, the business became all about me. I am the face of it. My website is nadiafiner.com—my face is all over it! Knowing that my mates, my neighbours or old work colleagues have seen me talking about business is just plain weird, but I'm not going to let a little bit of weird stop me building my empire.

In the past, I've worked with certain people whose approach to sales was more aggressive than a pack of hyenas ripping a zebra's carcass to shreds. Ewww. Seeing them stalk their prey, pin them down and intimidate them until they succumbed and signed on the dotted line freaked me out completely and sent me running for cover behind a tree. Surely selling doesn't need to be such a bloody mess?

There's a lot of sleaze out there. People using all kinds of dodgy techniques, like encouraging people to get into debt, manipulating them until they break down, or hounding them via email or even via phone until they cave. It's so full on.

I can't stand it. Surely you don't have to be all over people like a rash, or a customer service assistant in the GAP. Back off!

To avoid all this awkwardness, when I first started out, I developed a new, totally unique, and of course completely genius approach. I decided to avoid sales all together.

My plan was to make a bunch of stuff, so awesome that people would be bound to hear about my splendidness and come running towards me in their droves. I'd be so inundated I'd have to fend them off with a mini water cannon, or perhaps just a water pistol. This inventive method (which had nothing to do with my fear of sales and rejection) was going to make me millions.

It didn't work.

This method is flawed. You're relying on people to find you. Then you're relying on them to know how you can help them. Attraction marketing is all well and good if you're selling digital downloads or even low-priced courses, but what if you're selling a one-to-one service? There's no getting away from the fact that people are hiring you, and therefore they will probably need to actually have a conversation with you before they part with a few thousand dollars. Even with a stream of referrals, you still need to have sales conversations otherwise you end up letting warm leads wander off into the sunset.

If you're playing hard to get, I guess it could maybe work that your potential clients are so keen to reel you in that they're prepared to play chase. But what happens when someone else pops up who's actually prepared to talk to your potential client? Chances are you'll lose out.

It's time to grow a pair. Let's learn to sell without sleaze or sweat or shyness.

Selling is Helping

What if we re-frame the way we think about selling? Instead of trying to ram our stuff down people's throats, what if we take a step back. Instead of force-feeding our clients like some kind of twisted fois gras goose farmer, we could approach it differently. What if we think about selling as listening to our people, and then offering them the help they need?

As soon as I started to see sales in a different light, everything changed for me. Now it flows. It's easy. And it's a continuation of my desire to help people.

With this new attitude, all we need to do is talk to our people, listen to what they want, understand where they're heading and why they're stuck, and then if you're the best person to help them, offering to help them. It's a beautiful thing.

This shift has helped me no end. And it's cut down on my antiperspirant usage too.

Don't Be a Tease

Let's assume that your people need you. They do, right? Because you've listened to them and they've told you they do. But, instead of offering to help them, your awkwardness takes over and you shy away from closing the deal. You're leaving people disappointed. You got them all excited at the prospect of some action with you, and you've just let them go. Don't be a tease. Don't leave people hanging. They've got needs! And you're not meeting those needs. You've just kind of waved it in their face and not done the deal.

Selling to your people is not about you and your feelings of self worth. You have knowledge that they need. And by swerving away from the sale, you're not giving it to them.

Sales Conversations

Sales conversations are the backbone of your business. Unless you have regular sales calls, it's going to be hard to make money. Make them a priority and you'll create a regular stream of leads. And what do leads lead to? Clients, that's what!

Let's say you have two sales calls per week, eight per month. I wonder how many new clients you could land? Maybe three new clients a month? And say each client is worth $5000 to your business, that's $15k a month. That's off the back of making just two calls a week.

Why then, would you avoid sales conversations? Why would you choose instead to focus on stuff that might keep you occupied and may at some point lead to a sale at some point in the distant future? That would be crazy. You'll end up looking like you're doing great stuff, popping up everywhere on social media … but you won't be making money!

This is not a fancy scheme or formula. It's common sense! If you prioritize sales conversations, you have an immediate advantage over the competition who may not have cottoned on. If you create a consistent flow of sales calls, you'll have a consistent flow of clients. The rest of the stuff you could be doing is nice to have. This is the ultimate money making activity.

★ ★ ★ CASE STUDY: AMBER PHILLIPS ★ ★ ★
Amber Phillips is a web designer for creative entrepreneurs.
www.amberphillipsdesign.co.uk

Business was bumbling along. I was picking up a client every now and then but there wasn't much focus or clear direction. But instead of strategically trying strategies that would work for my target audience and sticking with them, I was being pulled in every direction. It was one big mess, and that's how I felt myself!

I felt like I should be making cold calls and going to networking events in order to be successful, but as an introvert I struggled so much with doing this. It made me feel like a complete failure. I didn't realise that when you run your own business, you can make your own rules, and that there are other ways to actively get clients without making the dreaded cold calls!

Since then I've made some huge shifts in my business and started offering discovery calls. Any type of call has always terrified me, but especially calls via Skype where you show your face! But now I'm able to push past my fears and have a valuable conversation with potential clients. I'd estimate around 80% of my discovery calls have resulted in a project. Even some of my first discovery calls where I'm sure I sounded like a stuttery mouse. I was ecstatic to receive an email shortly after giving the go-ahead for the project. I've even got a waiting list now! I never thought I'd get to that point when I first started my business.

Structure Your Sales Conversations

My first few discovery calls were a nightmare. I'd talk to anyone who expressed an interest in me, even if I knew they didn't have any money, or they were only interested in one of my entry-level products. The calls themselves were a farce. In my enthusiasm, desperate to be liked and feeling pressured to perform, I'd give away all my advice right there on the spot. I'd end up spending hours on the phone, then when it came to closing the deal I'd bottle it and just say goodbye.

It was not sustainable. (Read: it was a disaster.)

Over the years, I've honed my techniques and would you believe it, become pretty damn good at sales calls. I've even developed a sales script that I share with my clients. It helps them to steer the conversation, to structure it and to close the deal.

★ ★ ★ CASE STUDY: KARA GRANT ★ ★ ★
**Kara Grant, helps sensitive women to
unleash their sensitivity as their superpower.
www.soulconfidence.co.uk**

I could sell with ease from a stage, or via written messages but I struggled with selling through discovery calls. I never prioritized doing them because I didn't like them, and when I did get round to it, I would end up giving actual advice on the call, treating it more like a coaching session than a sales conversation. As a result, the person would feel overloaded with guidance and not be in the right place to make a decision. I think I felt like I would be a charlatan if I didn't give lots of value on the calls! It felt really clunky to be having a conversation about someone's pain and then hit them with a 'Now work with me!' all of a sudden, so I shied away from the actual selling bit at the end of the call.

So I got help with my discovery call technique, and it's changed everything. I've learned how to listen and how to use the right questions to allow the potential client to explore what they need. I now know that selling is not about you, it's about serving and sharing.

Learning how to support people on the call, and transition through the different stages of the sales conversation, has been fantastic. The first call I made, armed with my new skills, got me my highest paying client!

How to Sell

Sales calls, landing pages, email campaigns; however you sell, there are some simple ways to do it better.

The transaction

I hate owing people money. It hangs over me. I don't know what to do with myself until it's paid. Like, if I go for a pizza with friends and someone pays for me, I feel all awkward until I try to ram the money into their handbag. It's like there's something out of whack until I've paid my bills.

The same goes for your business. If you don't close the deal and ask for the sale, there's a strange imbalance. Like me and my pizza, your potential client feels odd, as if they owe you somehow, but they don't know how to repay you. By avoiding the sale you're making your clients feel uncomfortable, and that's not good.

Call to action

It's all very well creating content, but if you don't tell people what they should do to take it further, it's just so much bleh. Make it easy for people to take action when they've read your blog, watched your video or downloaded your freebie. People like to know what the logical next step is, and they're waiting for you to tell them. If you don't mention it and you kinda sneak off, like I used to, then they'll look around for what to do for about five seconds and then get distracted and go work with someone else.

It's up to you what your call to action is. If you know that discovery calls help you win clients, then optimise for them. Make your call to action an invitation to book a discovery call at the end of everything you do. It's nice to have people downloading your freebies and stuff, so you can build your list, but it's much quicker, and you'll make much more money, if you're getting people to book in for calls.

Sales pages

If you want people to hire you, your website can do a lot of the work for you. And yet I often see half-assed pages on people's sites that don't actually *sell* a service. They just tell the reader what it is and what's included, not how it's going to change their lives. That's facts, not sales.

In order to sell it, man, you need to explain how it's going to impact them. Don't just tell me what it is; tell me why I need it. Why do I need it right now? How I'm going to be transformed by it? Why are you the person to help me? The purpose of a sales page is to build trust and present a compelling case that will persuade the reader that they simply must have what you're offering.

I use a similar structure in sales pages as I do with my sales conversations. It's all about helping people go from where they are now to where they want to be, overcoming the challenges they're facing. It's all about selling the dream; how their life will be when they work with you.

Qualify your leads

You should not be having sales conversations with anyone and everyone. That would be a complete waste of your time. You should only be talking to people who have the time to get the benefit from what you're offering, the money to pay for it, and who are a good fit for your business. The purpose of a discovery call is to get to know each other better and find out the details of what the person needs help with, but you should already know something about them. You only want to be on calls with people who need your help and who have the money to pay you.

Follow up

Keep a record of leads (the people you've spoken to) and follow up with them. Even if they weren't quite ready to work with you when you spoke to them, it doesn't mean that you should just chuck them out into the wind and let them go. If you keep in touch and check in with them from time to time to see how they're getting on, they'll appreciate you showing that you care, and you'll be front of their mind when they are ready to go forwards.

Be The Boss

*a*re you the boss of your business? Or are you being a big wimp, hiding your light under the nearest bushel. You are a leader, whether you like it or not.

Maybe you don't wake up every morning thinking, yep, I'm a leader, what's the change I'm going to be today? But if so, why the heck not?

The Reluctant Boss

I wonder why we resist the idea of owning our greatness and stepping forth into the world, leading our tribe of people from the front. Ha. Of course I don't wonder why we resist it!

Being a leader means being seen. It's putting your ideas and yourself on the line. And it's exposing and scary.

I've always shied away from the spotlight. As a kid I never went on a stage. Ever. If I won a prize I'd hide in the loo, so I wouldn't have to get on the stage to get it.

My posture was terrible. I used to hunch over, like I was trying to shrink or hide away. I still have to make an effort to stand up straight. It's not like I'm tall!

When I worked in big companies I tended to skulk around. I remember in my first marketing role, the HR director telling me that I needed to raise my profile and to be more visible. I literally had no idea what he was on about. I was fairly sure he was insane, so I didn't pay any attention. I mean, I showed up for work each day. Did most of my work. He knew who I was. I had a bunch of cool buddies. What more did he want?

I still have a tendency to stand behind other people in photos. And rather than striding around the place like I own it, I often feel like I'm lurking in the background. At social occasions I get all awks if someone actually talks to me, and it takes me ages (or a few drinks) to warm up. And I swear I'm getting worse as I get older.

And yet, in this business they call business, when you create a personal brand, you are the star; the leader, the inspirer of people, the boss of it all. You can't creep around and hide. Well, not if you actually want to grow your business, you can't.

I know it's not that simple, and that often every pound of us resists it like mad. I mean, it's so unfair, (stamps feet) why can't we just get on with doing what we're doing and keep ourselves to ourselves?

Putting yourself out there in the big wide world is scary as hell. And that's why it's so tempting to hide. There are some tell-tale signs that you're hiding in your business.

- You use the 'royal we' when you talk about your business, pretending to be a bigger company than you really are. You're hiding! It may seem innocuous, but it's inauthentic and people can see through it.

- Your business videos and photos don't feature you, you avoid live streams and you use someone else as the face of your business. You're hiding!
- Your social media posts are bland and faceless marketing spiel. You're hiding! If you don't show any personality or commitment, almost as if you just feel you should be ticking the marketing box, then no wonder it's not working.

Given half the chance I would hide behind my computer, avoiding all kinds of visibility. I'd sit at home hoping clients would magically appear at my door, without having to do a thing. I mean, why would I take the risk of putting myself out there, in the open, for people to look at me, and have opinions about me? People might judge me. They might laugh at me. They may think I sound funny. I don't want to become some internet meme!

But that approach is not going to work.

It's time to make a change.

Because, unless you do, the people who you could be helping will never even find out about that help. Ultimately, it's not about you. I know it feels like it is, but if you wimp out, people are not getting what they need, and that's a damn shame for them.

You are the boss of your life and your business. It's time to step up.

The Questions People Ask When They're Hiding

What if people think I'm being bossy?

Being bossy is not a good thing, is it? Many of us may have even been told to rein it in. Having opinions or trying to change the status quo is seen as annoying and troublesome. Leadership qualities are not soft qualities. Leaders bang their fists on the table and tell people they're fired. And maybe that's why we step back. We don't want people to think we're full of ourselves or we like the sound of our voices. And bit by bit, our boss-iness is eroded.

But what if my friends and family think I'm weird?
You have to let go of the worry that your dad might see what you're doing on his Facebook. Maybe people from different areas of our life will be interested in what we're doing, or maybe they won't. Maybe they'll be inspired, or maybe they'll think you're a total loser. It doesn't really matter. The people who are meant to hear your message will hear you, and the people who are not interested will let it wash over them. If people care about you, and they love you, they'll be proud of you and want you to succeed, whether or not they're into what you're doing. And if they're slagging you off behind your back, then may I suggest they're not worth hanging around with.

But what if some people don't like me?
We want people to like us. And the idea that some people might not be that into you feels weird. But the fact is, if you're just being you, and you're being you in the fullest most you way possible, some people are gonna love you and some people will be a bit … meh. And that's OK. You don't want everyone to like you, believe me. Middle of the road is boring, and beige. And you're not bland. You're fabulous. And that's why it's OK for some people not to like you. Our goal is to attract our ideal clients, only. And everyone else can jog on (in the nicest possible way).

But what if I look silly?
You know what you're doing, right? Of course you do. You've trained for this for ages. You've got skills. So why would you look silly?

The voices in your head saying this stuff are just trying to keep you safely locked up at home where you can't come to any harm. (They're the idiots, because we all know that most injuries happen in the home!)

If you're going to go big with this business of yours then we're going to need to put those doubts and insecurities to one side. Thank them for their concern and then press on regardless.

Personally, I like to embrace the silly. Whenever I do a live stream, mad stuff happens. Like I get a sneezing fit. Or a fly will land on my head. Or the postman arrives with a delivery for my neighbour. Or the dog barks at the wind (probably his own). Rather than allow these things to derail or even devastate me, I just laugh at them (and usually at myself) and crack on.

Enough of the what-ifs!

Be a Warrior Not a Worrier

Let me tell you a little story. Brie has got it going on. She has skills many of us can only dream of. She's awesome.

But right now, she's keeping it to herself. Not because she's being selfish (although ultimately she is being selfish…) but, because she's scared. Scared of being seen.

The mere thought of putting herself out there frightens the living crap out of her. When she thinks about pushing herself, charging more, offering something different, standing on a stage, making videos she gets scared. She's always been shy and has never been one to put herself forward for things or shout about her own skills.

Instead of doing the thing she knows she was put on this planet to do, she gets stuck, and starts bumbling around. On a good day she'll just fiddle around on Facebook, looking for a quick win. On a bad day she'll come up with a whole new business idea that she's convinced she should follow instead because it means she doesn't have to face up to the fact that she's hiding.

Doing something easy and simple and safe is really flippin' attractive when you've got the fear. But those things don't make you any money.

I get it. I really do. In fact as I was writing this, it struck me that I do all those things! Fear and I, we go way back. I get the fear a lot. When I'm launching. When I'm selling. When I'm travelling the world giving talks. When I'm being interviewed on podcasts. When I'm sitting down to write. All the time. Going big is scary. It makes me want to run and hide. I wobble. A lot. It often takes every inch of my inner strength to slap my fears down.

But I've realized that when I let fear get the better of me, I can't help people. I get stuck in busy work and I stop being able to help my clients. If I fall at the final hurdle and wimp out of telling people what I do and showing them how I can help them, I'm leaving them in the lurch.

I took Brie out for waffles (banoffee, in case you were wondering. And no, not gluten free). While we ate, she admitted she was scared of going big in her business. She was worried people would judge her, not like her, or think she was talking a load of crap. And that was why she was avoiding doing the important stuff. And she was sabotaging her chances of success.

I encouraged Brie to be the boss of her business. To focus on what she does best and stop doing random stuff that isn't going to make her any money. I showed her that going BIG doesn't need to be scary. By shifting the focus away from how she feels about herself and concentrating on the people she loves to help, it suddenly didn't seem so scary. And who knows, if people actually see her, she might get some new clients!

If you're hiding because you're scared, it's time to let it go. You owe it to yourself to move past your fears, to pick yourself up, get it together and be the boss. Then you can get out there and turn your business into the success you know it can be.

When you let the idea of scaling your business freeze you in your tracks, and you keep yourself small, you're depriving people of your magic.

And when you've made it out to the other side, you'll look back on what you've achieved and it will feel amazing! Believe me.

What Does It Mean to Be a Leader?

A leader has a vision for how they'd like the world to be, and usually that involves challenging the status quo and bringing about change. But rather than setting off on some big ego trip to do it all on their own, a leader takes their tribe with them on the journey. A leader is dedicated to the people they help, because they're passionate about making a change for those people.

We all have it in us to be a leader. The question is though, do you have the guts to get up off your butt and do something about it?

The Beta Boss

What if we could embrace our quietness or our shyness and become an authentic, honest, real leader who still inspires our people and leads our business from the front?

We can.

Being a leader is not about acting how you think a leader should be. No shoulder pads or killer heels required, unless of course that's a look you love. Your people don't want you to be anyone other than you. And that means, if you're a quiet kind of a person, or you're super modest, or a bit socially awkward, that's the kind of leader you'll be. And that's OK.

Your people need you

If there's something that needs sorting, you owe it to your people to stand up and get it sorted. How you feel about being seen, or how scared you are of leadership, is far less important. If the way things are just isn't working, then someone has to step up and sort it—and that someone is you. Letting your doubts and insecurities get in the way is not an option. Your people need you.

I wonder what the impact could be on your people, and your business, if you got up from behind your computer (or this book) and stepped forward as a leader of your tribe.

Beyond the business

But trying to be a leader by just shouting, "Buy my stuff! Buy my stuff!" isn't going to get a lot of traction. Leading a tribe is about more than your bottom line, although it will ultimately drive sales It's about your message, and bringing about a change in the world.

Have something to say. Rail against the way things are. Desire change. Have a point of view and own it. Don't shy away from what you really think. If you go in and you're all, like, meh. Nobody is going to give a crap about you and your business. If you have a strong message then people's ears are going to prick up when you talk.

I get very frustrated when I see business owners playing small. It drives me nuts when people have had the courage get their own business off the ground, only for their fears and limiting beliefs to keep them small. We are so lucky! There is literally nothing stopping us from turning our tiny one-woman-band of a business into something huge. The only thing in our way, is us. And I'm on a mission to do something about it.

That's what I stand for. What do you and your business stand for?

Be open

People hire people. They want to get to know you, the real you. And frankly, if it's just you in your business, there's no getting away from this. People will want to know about why you're doing what you do. And that's why you're going to tell your story. It's the backbone of your brand.

At first I wasn't so keen to tell people the truth. I wanted to present a shiny version of myself to the world to show I knew what I was doing.

But once I finally got the guts to write my story and talk openly about the challenges I've faced, my lack of confidence and how I've held myself back, people really started to connect with me.

Lead by example

Be the change. Show your people that you're doing it by sharing your journey and the things you've experienced. By demonstrating what's possible, you're putting an inspiring vision in front of them, something that excites and scares them a little at the same time, and because you've done it they'll trust you to take them with you to get there.

Be outrageously you

No matter what you might think of their opinions or their methods, great leaders are never dull. If you hold back because you're worried about being too out there, you risk being super forgettable and turning everyone off. March to the beat of your own drum. If you're a bit weird, then be a bit weird. Let it all hang out.

Go niche

You know who your ideal clients are (or you should, if you've been paying attention so far). You are going to be the leader of this tribe, a tribe made up of your ideal clients. It doesn't matter if it's very niche, related to a specific subculture. If you're leading a movement of people who want to knit their own underwear—go with it. Make it super clear who you're for, who your tribe are and why. When you do this, you attract the right kind of people. If you struggle to connect, imagine you're talking to one person, your ideal person. Maybe you know who that person is. Talk to their fears, their concerns, their passions, their desires. Just chat to them like they're your good friend.

Shout about it

It's not enough to just write your message and your story on your website. It's not enough to work out what you stand for and what you believe in, and write it in your planner and make it look all pretty. You have to own your message and shout it from the rooftops. Imagine you're a politician; it's not enough to just get a couple of posters printed and then sit and home and wonder if people are going to vote for you.

Get off your butt cheeks. Get out there and be seen by your people. Stop making excuses.

I've made plenty of those myself, so I know when you're doing it. If you hide behind your computer, it's impossible for you to build trust.

I don't think you can ever really do this too much. (Except perhaps at family gatherings, or friends' birthday parties.) Keep it relevant and target your ideal kind of people, and then really go for it.

Consistency is crucial

Keep your message consistent. I'm not saying you should repeat yourself over and over, because that could get dull very quickly. Instead, make sure what you're talking about ties back into your key message. Whether you're talking about just one aspect of what you do, giving some general tips or talking about your journey, make sure you keep on message.

One half-hearted blog post isn't going to cut it I'm afraid. Choose what suits you best and do it a lot. If you love video, do that. If you're a talker, podcast. If you're a writer, write blogs and emails to your people. Concentrate your efforts. Don't spread yourself too thinly. I'd rather you rocked Facebook and left Twitter and Instagram alone, if it meant doing Facebook really, really well. Hang where your people are hanging. The rest is just a waste of your time.

The lazy sloth in all of us wants to think that this isn't true, but I've tested it, and doing it daily will have a big impact on your results. Look around you; successful people in your field are doing it. They get in front of people, often.

Work out what's possible in the time you have available, and aim to be consistent. Don't make it into a massive full-on pain in the butt. It needs to be something you can do with joy and lightness in your heart because this is how you get to connect with your peeps. If you make it fun so you actually like doing it, people will be able to tell and you'll get better results. If it's clear you hate every minute of it, they will ditch you.

Beyond Bragging

If you don't own your expertise, why would anyone believe in you? Nobody is going to believe in a leader who's all, like, actually I'm a bit rubbish.

But that doesn't mean you have to boast. Rather than big myself up and get firmly wedged up my own butt, I leverage testimonials from happy clients and members of my tribe. I'd much rather have honest reviews do the talking for me. You too can easily collect together the nice things people have said about you and spread them about. It's the perfect solution; the perfect way to cement your authority without getting all embarrassed.

Believe it, baby

Stepping into your power as a leader can bring about big changes, believe me. It might sound like madness, all this talk of global movements and going big, but it is possible.

Of course it's scary. But we're not going to let fear get in our way are we? You owe it to your people. They need you and your message. They need your help. And if you're at home hiding in your dressing gown then you're not going to be helping anyone are you?

The difference between someone who goes full boss on their business and someone who holds back? Choice. It's up to you.

You can do this. No more hiding. No more playing small. You are a total ninja.

★ ★ ★ CASE STUDY: JANE PIKE ★ ★ ★
**Jane Pike, founder of horse riding
coaching service Confident Rider.
www.confidentrider.online**

The one thing that I was clear on right from the beginning was that I wanted my business to reflect my own thoughts and opinions. But I had this idea that being professional meant being faceless. The content I was sharing was valuable but there was no personality behind it. My first website was a mass of stock images and you would have had to search hard to find a picture of me. It lacked soul and fun.

The problem is the more personal you are, the more 'you' your work is, the more vulnerable you feel. But I now realize that that vulnerability is where the real gold is; you have to be brave enough to show up if you expect your clients to do the same. I realized that I owed it to the people who might consider working with me to show them what I am about, to be available, so that they consider me approachable and on their team.

I remember watching a vlog and deciding I had to do one too., I made a pact with myself to do one vlog a week for the next year. Posting the first one was horrendous! I had hot flashes and was convinced everyone would think I was a giant douchebag. The only blank wall available was a pokey little space under a heat pump, and the wall was a weird peach color. I filmed from my laptop so the quality was grainy, and it used to take me hours to do a single vlog. I look at them now and want to hide under a pillow! But I stuck to it.

I would say that my level of visibility is hugely responsible for where I am today. I blog and vlog regularly, and it's the single most important thing I do. I'm on Facebook live a couple of times a week. I'm invested in the people who follow me. I really like them, learn loads from them and want to help where I can. I love hanging out in my online spaces. It's a good time in there!

Being visible builds relationships and trust. When I teach or hold seminars, people talk to me like they know me already. They feel like they do! It creates a level intimacy and trust that you can really build on, and allows you to skim over the small talk and get straight to the good stuff!

I never imagined I'd be leading a tribe. It's quite surreal, but it really excites me. I have so much I want to do and share, it's only onwards and upwards from here.

CONCLUSION

To Bigness and Beyond

Wow! I bet you're feeling all buzzy and fuzzy right now. So many thoughts and ideas bouncing around your brain, it's like you've just had a mega binge at the all you can eat business buffet. If you're anything like me after a big ideas-fest, you're probably unable to move a muscle, let alone leap up and take action.

In case you've gone all blurry or completely blank, here's a quick reminder of what we've covered.

I've taken you step by step down the Profit Path and shown you how to scale your business in the simplest, least stressiest way possible. I've shown you that it is possible to build a global business in just a few hours a day, from your sofa. That it's possible to be a lone ranger, and go global, even if your working day is briefer than a good brunch. I've shown you that running a big business does not mean getting swamped by investors, premises, employees and all that jazz.

I've shown you how to create a big impact in your business, whilst fitting your business around your life, not take it over. Just because you are your business and your business is you, there's no reason to poop all over your profits. A tiny business can be perfectly formed, and very powerful.

I've shown you how to go from making a few dollars each month to creating a little big business, one that impacts thousands of lives, with clients all over the world and a consistent stream of income. No more playing small, and working all the hours for tiny profits. I've shown you how to go big in your business, without hassle or hustle.

There will be no more playing small. You're going to kick fear in the face and turn your tiny profits into big bucks.

By following the Profit Path, I've grown my business from making a few dollars a month into a global brand with clients all over the world, and a very healthy and consistent stream of income… all whilst having the time to do the school run, walk the dog, see my friends, go to boxing and have a nap in the middle of the day if I feel like it.

These are the exact steps I've used to help my clients reach $5K months, then $20K months and beyond. They too have been able to stop playing small and get out of their own way. I've helped them get over their fears, create a unique brand, attract long term loving clients who pay them properly, create recurring streams of revenue, and fall back in love with their businesses.

These are the steps you can take right now; to scale up your business and go from working all the hours for tiny profits, to creating a little big business; a global business of one!

This stuff that really works. It may not be a shiny blueprint or a complex formula, but it works. Man I wish I'd had something like this all those years ago. I would have saved myself a helluva lotta hassle and heartache.

I know it's a lot to take in. So, if you've completely forgotten what to do first, here's a reminder. Here's exactly what you can do right now to scale your business, like right now.

1. BIG VISION

    Get clear on where you're going and sort your head out to increase your chances of getting there. Focus on what works and ditch the rest.

2. BIG PERSONALITY

    Be authentic and real. Discover what makes you unique so you can stand out from the crowd. Do you.

3. BIG LOVE

    Work out who your perfect people are, understand what they really want, and build long lasting loving relationships with them.

4. BIG PROFIT

    Design your business and the way you work to make more money! Create packages and group programs to leverage your time and expertise. Outsource and automate so you can focus on what you do best.

5. BIG IMPACT

    Prioritize sales in your business—and realize that selling is just helping. Own your expertise and be the boss of your business.

It's as simple as that. 5 simple steps to follow that will enable you to scale up and make more money in your business.

I've shown you exactly what to do and I've shown you that it's possible. I mean, if I can do this, and my clients have done this, then so can you.

YOU can do this.

But, now it's over to you. It's action time!

I wish I could tell you that just by clicking your heels together, sprinkling fairy dust or going for a ride in the Delorian, you'll be transported to a more profitable shiny future. It doesn't quite work like that. Don't expect change overnight. But, if you follow these steps. You too can go from scraping by to creating a thriving business, a global brand, and a constant flow of lovely clients.

The secret though is action. You have to take the first step. It's not enough to read this book and then stuff it in the bottom of your bag and expect change to take place via osmosis. You have to do stuff.

And that's the scary bit.

I get it. Change is daunting. Particularly when every ounce of your being is telling you to leave well alone. I mean, what if this actually worked? Then life would be different in all kinds of ways, and that's scary in itself. You'd be facing the unknown. And that's terrifying.

But if you want life and business to be different and better, you have to do something about it. A little at a time.

I'm not advocating you race up the steps and leap off the top diving board, arms flailing right away. But if you take one step at a time… and inch your way closer, day by day… you'll get there in the end.

Only a small percentage of entrepreneurs reading this book will take action. The majority will just add another notch on their business book bedpost. I know what that's like. I have my very own mini library!

The thing is, having a library is not the same as actually making changes.

And what makes us make a change? If we want something that's what. I want to shift a few lbs… so I'm drinking herbal tea as I write this. I'd love to chugging down hot chocolate, but I know that if I want to fit into my skinny jeans that's a big no no. The vision of me looking like a boss in my boxing gear is what keeps me taking action and choosing the chai!

Right. Let's take a moment to think about how things could be different in your business. Let's imagine you take the first step today. What could your business be like in say six months? How would you spend your days? Would you be working with lovely clients all over the world? Would you have a buzzing group program? Would you have a virtual assistant taking care of all your admin? Would you have a diary filled with discovery calls?

What would you be earning? What would you be able to do with all that extra money? How would that make you feel?

Pretty good right?!

But you have to take action. If you choose to let fear win, nothing is going to change in your business. It's as simple as that.

And you're better than that, right?

Let's do this!

I've loaded you up with as much information and advice as I possibly can. But, I get that it's not always easy to make big changes on your own. If you're worried that I've opened up the doors to a new way of working, but you don't feel you can do it alone.

Don't worry.

That's why I've created the Profit Pack to help you move forwards with me holding your hand every step of the way.

The Profit Pack provides all the support you need to go from tiny profits to achieving consistent $5K months. You can find out more information and sign up to join the next time the doors open here **www.nadiafiner.com/pack**

If you'd like to go VIP and work with me more closely on your business, on a one to one basis, I'd like to invite you to book in for a breakthrough call with me here **ww.nadiafiner.com/call**

And as for me?

Writing this book has been a huge leap for me. I'm so proud that I've done it! And as a result, I'm going to be able to help thousands of entrepreneurs to turn their tiny businesses into big bucks.

Yes, it's been scary, but every time I've stepped up, my business has blossomed as a result, with more and more exciting opportunities coming my way. I've got big plans to continue speaking all over the world ... and recording more podcasts... and of course continuing to work with my lovely clients and helping them to go from tiny profits to a Little Big Business.

I'm looking forward to hearing about your journey to creating a little big business. I'd love to hear from you, don't be shy, so why not pop over to Facebook and tell me all about it! **www.facebook.com/nadiafiner**.

Here's to going big, and taking over the world, in our pajamas.

Nadia xx

About the Author

Nadia Finer is one of the UK's most foremost business coaches with ten years' experience supporting female entrepreneurs in her own unique style. She has helped hundreds of clients around the world to start and grow their businesses, specializing in helping clients work less and make more money. Nadia is a published author, renowned speaker and podcaster. Nadia lives in London with her husband, son Jacob and fuzzy dog, Bobby.

www.nadiafiner.com

Morgan James
Speakers Group

www.TheMorganJamesSpeakersGroup.com

We connect Morgan James published authors with live and online events and audiences who will benefit from their expertise.

 Morgan James makes all of our titles available
through the Library for All Charity Organization.

www.LibraryForAll.org

Printed in the USA
CPSIA information can be obtained
at www.ICGtesting.com
JSHW022334140824
68134JS00019B/1473

9 781683 508519